MW01351707

Published by
Texas Fish & Game Publishing Co., L.L.C.

1745 Greens Road
Houston Texas 77032
Phone: 281-227-3001
Website: www.fishgame.com

101 Freshwater Kayak Launching Points

by Paul Batchelder, Sr.

First Edition

Edited by Roy Neves

Cover and book design by Wendy Kipfmiller-O'Brien

All photos by Paul Batchelder, Sr.

ISBN: 978-0-9908415-0-0

101 FRESHWATER KAYAK LAUNCHING POINTS

Detailed, accurate directions, photos and other helpful information on 101 places to launch Kayaks, Canoes and other boats in Texas freshwater lakes and rivers.

We ended up with more locations than expected and we have included them all in this book.

Well over 101 actual locations for you to explore.

BY PAUL BATCHELDER, SR.

CONTENTS

Safety

Safety First ... 1

Etiquette

Mind Your Manners ... 5

Fishing Thoughts

... 7

THE WATER

Houston Urban 9

Sheldon Reservoir ... 10
Greens Bayou Park ... 12
Armand Bayou in Bay Area Park ... 14
Challenger 7 Park ... 16
Riverside Inn Marina on the San Jacinto River ... 18

Buffalo Bayou 21

Hwy 6 ... 22
Memorial Mews ... 24
Dairy Ashford ... 26
West Sam Houston Tollway ... 28
Briar Bend ... 30
Woodway/Memorial Launch ... 32
Hogg Bird Sanctuary ... 34
Eleanór Tinsley Park ... 36
Sabine Street ... 38
Allen's Landing ... 40

Houston East 43

McCullum Park ... 44
Hugo Park ... 46
Gou Hole ... 48

TABLE OF CONTENTS

Trinity River Island/Wallisville Lake Project 50
Trinity River I-10 W. East & West 52
River Terrace Park 54

Lake Houston 57

Luce Bayou, Ponderosa Ramp 58
BJ's Marina 60
Alexander Deussen Park 62

Lake Woodlands 65

North Shore Park 66

Lake Conroe 69

FM 830 Ramp 70
Cagle Launch 72
Stubblefield Ramp 74
Scotts Ridge 76

Lake Raven 79

Huntsville State Park 80

Kurth Lake 83

Kurth Lake Launch 84

Trinity River North 87

Trinity River on Highway 59 88
Riverside 90
Harmon Creek Marina, 14 Marina Point Drive 92

Lake Pinkston 95

Lake Pinkston Dam 96
Lake Pinkston East 98

Lake Nacogdoches 101

Lake Nacogdoches, Eastside Park 102
Lake Nacogdoches, Westside Park 102

Neches River North 105

Anderson Crossing CR 1155 106
Highway 7 108

BA Steinhagen Lake 111

West Side of the Lake:
Magnolia Ridge Park 112
Magnolia 1 112
Magnolia 2 113
Campers Cove Park 114
Cherokee 1 116
Cherokee 2 118
East Side of the Lake:
Tidelands Ramp 120
Walnut Ridge 122
Hen House Ridge 124
Hen House Canoe Launch 125
Sandy Creek Park 126
Sandy Creek 1 Kayak/Canoe 127
Sandy Creek 2 128
Sandy Creek 3 129
Sandy Creek 4 130

Big Thicket, Village Creek, Lower Neches 133

FM 418 Launch Village Creek 134
FM 327 Launch Village Creek 136
Baby Galvez Launch Village Creek 138
Hwy 96 Crossing Village Creek 140
Village Creek State Park 142
Pine Island Bayou Launch 146
LNVA Saltwater Barrier 147
Collier's Ferry Park 148
Evadale Launch Neches River 150
County Park Launch 152
Cleveland/105 Launch 154

Colorado River 157

Columbus, Texas Launch Sites 158
SH 71 Business 159
Beasons Park 160
Hollywood Park 162
521 River Park 164
Hanson Riverside Park on the San Bernard River 166

Fayette County Reservoir 169

Oak Thicket 170
Park Prairie 172

Lake Somerville 175

Birch Creek State Park 176
Big Creek Park Marina Private 178
Overlook Marina Private 179
Rocky Creek Park 180
Yegua Creek Park (1) 181
Yegua Creek Park (2) 182
Welch Park 183
Iron Bridge 184
Nails Creek State Park 185

Lake Livingston 187

Wolf Creek Park 188
Indian Creek Launch 189
Blanchard 190
Tigerville Park 191
Waterfront Lodge 192
Double Lake 193
Point Adventure Bridge 194
356 Marina 195
Cauthin Park 196
Patrick's Ferry 197
Point Blank 198

Spring & Cypress Creeks 199

Collins Park 202
Kuykendahl 204
Pundt Park 206
Riley Fuzzel 208
Carter Park 209
Cypresswood Drive Bridge 210
Jesse H. Jones Park & Nature Center 211
Edgewater San Jacinto River 212

Brazos River/Simonton 215

1093 Launch 216
FM 1489 Mullins Crossing 218

Lake Texana 221

Hwy 172 Launch 222
County Road 237 Launch 223
Hwy 111 Launch 224
Breckenridge Complex Ramp 7 225
Hwy 59 Ramp 4 226
Hwy 59 Ramp 3 227

Victoria 229

Riverside Boat Ramp 230
Pumphouse 1201 Stayton Ave. 231

Guadalupe River 233

Max Starcke Park 234
Lake Placid (I-10) 235
Rivershade RV Park 236

Goliad 237

San Antonio River at Hwy 59 238
Ferry Street 239
Goliad State Park 240

Boerne and Coleto Creek 243

Boerne City Lake 244
Coleto Creek 246

dedication

To Judy:

My wife, best friend, grandma, and trusted soul mate.
I thank God for you every day.
You always seem to give me the advice I need, just when I need it.
Your love and support, keeps me going.
Keep up the good work, we have a long way to go.

SAFETY

Safety First

Let me start by saying that the research for this book took more than a year. I have worked hard to find, and provide you the most accurate, detailed information possible.

Conditions change. In Texas things can change on an hourly basis.

Please use common sense when you are choosing a place on the water to fish or enjoy a paddle. If it looks unsafe do not attempt to launch.

Paddle in water that is suited for your ability. If you are just getting started you should consider distance and water flow very carefully, Remember this is supposed to be fun.

Always wear a PFD (Personal Flotation Device). No excuses.

Carry a whistle (it's the law) and a small knife. If you attach them to your PFD, you will always have them with you. When you need them, you really need them.

If you don't like a big life jacket, get one of the inflatable ones. They may cost a bit more, but guess what: YOU are worth it.

Make sure your boat and other equipment are in good working order. I am kind of a minimalist, so I do not carry a spare paddle or a ton of fishing equip. Bring what makes you happy.

Make sure what you DO bring is of good quality and well taken care of.

Paddle with someone, or be sure someone knows where you are and how long you expect to be out. If you go alone, always keep in touch with someone.

If you plan to be out early morning or late into the evening be sure to get a lighting system for your boat. You want to be seen.

Give way to the power boats. If you paddle in an area where there are lots of boats just know that sooner or later someone in a PB (power boat) is not going to see you until he is right on top of you. Just be prepared and be visible. On a lake you can see them from a long way off, on rivers and creeks you can hear them coming. If need be, get out of the way.

Take care of yourself. You can get all the mad you want later—when you are safe.

If it has been raining for days, use your head. Try one of the many lake launches and let the rivers and bayous calm down. Flash floods and high water can happen in a hurry in the smaller creeks and bayous. Check the weather before you go. Storms can travel quickly.

Don't risk getting caught in a bad situation.

Don't mess with Mother Nature.

He Lived to Tell His Story

THIS IS AN actual story of how fast things can change, as told by the man who fortunately lived to tell about it. It happened in March 2014. This was shared with his permission.

> **I HADN'T FISHED** in a few weeks due to being busy. So after enjoying a nice day on the San Jacinto River Saturday, I decided to not worry about the weather and headed to Cagle Park on Sunday. I arrived there around 10 a.m. It was cloudy, the water was flat and the wind was very

light. I paddled out in Lake Conroe, to the 1375 bridge and beyond, fishing.

After a few hours, I felt a very cold breeze on my neck, so I decided to head back. I crossed under the bridge, and the water got very choppy. There was another boat close by, but I decided to tough it up and not call for help.

The boat left and *bam*—the water got super choppy, and I capsized.

I attempted to self- rescue, but the kayak kept flipping on top of me. I am not sure if it was me panicking, due to water temperature, or the water conditions. I stayed with the kayak, but I felt like the current was carrying me to the middle of the lake.

So I made the decision to ditch the kayak and started swimming back. It crossed my mind to lose my rain jacket, life jacket, and pants to swim better, but I think if I had done that I probably wouldn't be here today.

After being in the water for close to an hour and numerous attempts to call for help with no luck, (I had my phone in a waterproof case on me), I yelled for help, and people in the campground heard me. They sent a boat and called an ambulance.

One gentleman was nice enough to get my kayak that drifted off about two miles. I lost all my gear, but I learned a pretty valuable lesson to always respect the weather and always wear my life jacket. I think carrying a whistle would have been beneficial too.

Things I did right:

- I had my PFD on.
- I carried my cellphone on me.
- I kept my keys on me and had a change of clothes in the car.

- I did not try to swim to the closest point. Instead I tried to swim with the current/wind and drift slowly to a close shore point.
- I abandoned my kayak, since I failed to self-rescue and noticed it drifting farther to the middle of the lake. I think if I was in the ocean, I would have never abandoned my kayak.

Things I did wrong:

- Ignored the weather conditions that day.
- Did not go with a buddy and did not notify anyone of my whereabouts. I first called 911 but the wind was too strong for them to understand me.
  Then I attempted to text a friend for help, and he assumed it was a prank.
- Did not carry a knife on me, I had it lying in my kayak. At one point I felt the fishing line and anchor rope wrap around my leg and had no way to cut it.
- Did not carry an air horn or whistle. I assumed that I am a good swimmer, and I am not that far from shore.

Be safe out there.

ETTIQUETTE

Mind Your Manners

Pick up after yourself and someone else. It breaks my heart to see the trash left around many of the launch sites I have visited. Just do your part, and if it's your trash take it with you. If you have a mind to, pick up some extra. I will say most kayakers I have met, appreciate the outdoors and our environment. They work to help keep it cleaned up.

If that's you, Thanks. Keep it up.

Don't fish on top of someone else. Again, just use common sense, which unfortunately is not all that common today. If someone is already fishing in your "secret spot" go find a new one until they leave. There is nothing I love better than fishing behind someone and catching a big fish.

Trust me, they will be watching you. There is always plenty of water—use it.

Use the golden rule, and do unto others as you would have them do to you.

Alligators do not eat people. I have had people tell me they would not fish an area because it had alligators. That's OK by me—less fishing pressure. I enjoy watching them, and the few times I have got close to them, they slip under the water and make their exit.

Just like every other wild animal I know, they do not want

anything to do with people. But just like any wild critter, if you choose to pester it, corner it, or mess with it when it has babies, or give it no way to get away, it will defend itself.

So enjoy watching them, photograph, them, but give them some space. Use good judgment and don't drag a stringer of fish behind your kayak when you are fishing in a place where gators are.

One of the great benefits of kayaking is you will encounter all kinds of wildlife along the riverbanks and lake shores. Respect their space and enjoy the show.

FISHING THOUGHTS

I WILL TELL you up front, I am no expert fisherman.

But if experience counts for anything, I have been at it for a while.

I grew up on the shores of one of the finest deep water lakes in the northeast, Lake Champlain. With several older brothers as mentors and guides, I spent many hours fishing year-round in this lake. We fished from the shore and in boats in the summer. We chased tip-ups and jigging sticks, fishing through the ice in winter.

Yellow perch, smallmouth, walleye, rock bass and northern pike were all familiar targets.

As I have grown older I have had the chance to fish some of the greatest places on God's green earth. Alaska, Hawaii, Colorado, Texas, Louisiana, Alabama, Mississippi, Montana, Utah, Yellowstone, the Caribbean, Tennessee, and yes, back in Vermont.

I have fly fished, surf fished, fished with ultralights and 14-foot-long rods. Spin cast, bait cast, cane pole, and yes, even a snoopy pole.

I have fished in creeks you could jump across and in salt water 40 miles off shore.

I like to fish. And I *really* like to fish from my kayak.

They say every fisherman goes through four fishing stages in his life;

First you just want to catch a fish.

Then you want to catch lots of fish.

Then you want to catch a really big fish.

And last you want to catch fish the way *you* want to catch fish.

I can honestly say I have been through all four—more than once. But now I do like to catch fish the way I want to catch them. I am a top water fan. When I fly fish, I like to use foam flies that I have tied, so I can watch the strike.

For bass, I like weedless frogs and buzz baits. In saltwater, I use spook-type baits and soft plastics.

I have a handful of baits that I use most of the time, now.

Confidence baits—I know they work, and I know how to fish them. Oh yeah, and I know that they will catch fish.

No matter what stage you find yourself in, enjoy it.

Be a good steward of our resources. Obey the fishing regulations. If you don't agree with the limits on size or numbers, get involved and change them.

If you are going to eat the fish you catch, enjoy them. If not, release them promptly.

Most of all, have fun.

HOUSTON URBAN

THERE ARE FIVE launch sites profiled in the area within a short distance from central Houston.

Sheldon Reservoir 10

Greens Bayou Park 12

Armand Bayou in Bay Area Park 14

Challenger 7 Park 16

Riverside Inn Marina 18

Sheldon Reservoir

8674 Pineland Road.

N 29 51.134, W 95 10.415 **Elevation: 44 feet**

From the intersection of Sam Houston Parkway (Beltway 8) east and Garret Road, go east on Garret for .5 miles to Pineland Rd. Turn right 2.5 miles. The reservoir and parking lot will be on the left. You can also access this from Hwy 90, east of Beltway 8. Turn north on Pineland Rd. The

launch will be on the right, .5 mile. This is a free, paved launch with a small parking lot.

If you are looking for a spot for a great paddle close to the city, this is it. The 1,254-acre reservoir was created in 1943 and offers a series of channels and islands that give you lots to explore. If you love birds this is a prime nesting spot for many species. Large-mouth bass, crappie, bluegill and catfish are all present in the lake. I have fished mainly for bass. Bring your weedless gear. Top water frogs and buzz baits will work well. The lily pads are abundant and make great cover for the bass. The water is clear to slightly stained. Calm water most of the time makes this a great place to paddle, because the flow is controlled water levels remain very consistent.

No amenities here. Be sure and take everything you need.

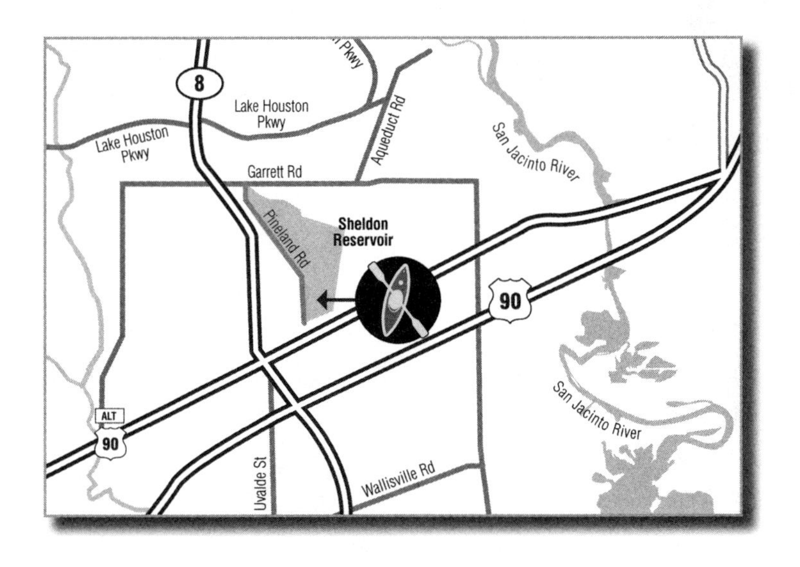

Greens Bayou Park

700 Westmont St. Houston

N 29 46.673, W 95 11.866 Elevation: 1 foot

From the intersection of Sam Houston Parkway (Beltway 8) east and I-10 east, travel west on I-10 and exit Uvalde. Continue west on the feeder road to Westmont Street. Turn right (north) and follow Westmont about .5 miles through this neighborhood. Greens Bayou Park will be on your left. At the time of my visit Feb. 2014, no formal launch was in place

Grass banks along the bayou will make for an

easy launch. Parking is available along the street. If the gate is open, you can pull right to the water's edge. If not you will have to portage about 100 yards across the field. The day I was here, the chain gate was not in place. The bayou is nice and wide here. Understand you are getting close to commercial boat traffic and heavy industrial use of the bayou. As with any bayou or small river, conditions can change in a hurry. Sadly there is a lot of trash accumulated along the banks here. The water in this area is very muddy—what you would expect in the lower sections of a bayou. No amenities at this location.

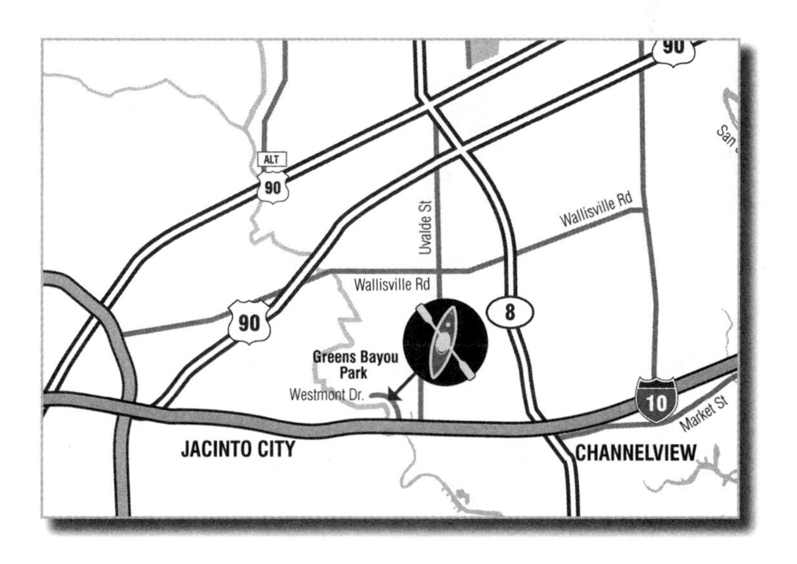

Armand Bayou in Bay Area Park

Bay Area Park 7500 E Bay Area Blvd., Houston

N 29 35.894, W 95 04.461 Elevation: 8 feet

FROM BELTWAY 8 and Red Bluff in Pasadena continue east on Red Bluff, 7.7 miles to Bay Area Boulevard. Turn right on Bay Area Blvd., 1.2 miles, the park is on the left. This is a free, paved launch. They also have a floating pier.

The park is open from 7 am to 10 pm.

Armand Bayou

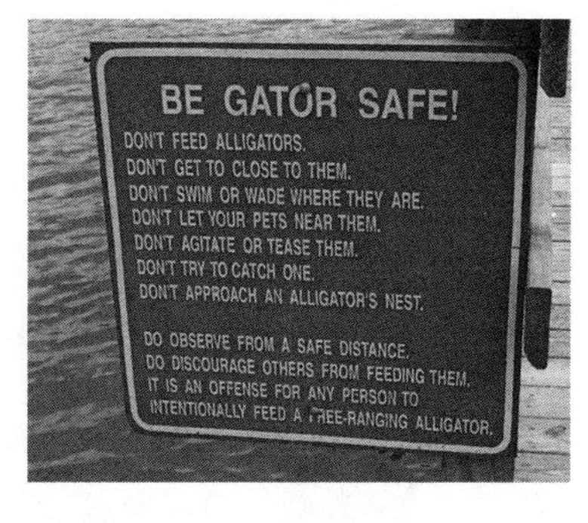

is a time-honored and treasured paddle spot. It is an official Texas Paddle Trail location. The bayou feeds southwest into Clear Lake. Wind can be an issue as the bayou widens. This is a must-try spot for anyone near 45 south. Brackish water will offer you a chance on catch anything from large blue cats to drum, bass, or speckled trout. The park has public rest rooms. It also has picnic areas and BBQ pits. A fenced, dog walking area is also available.

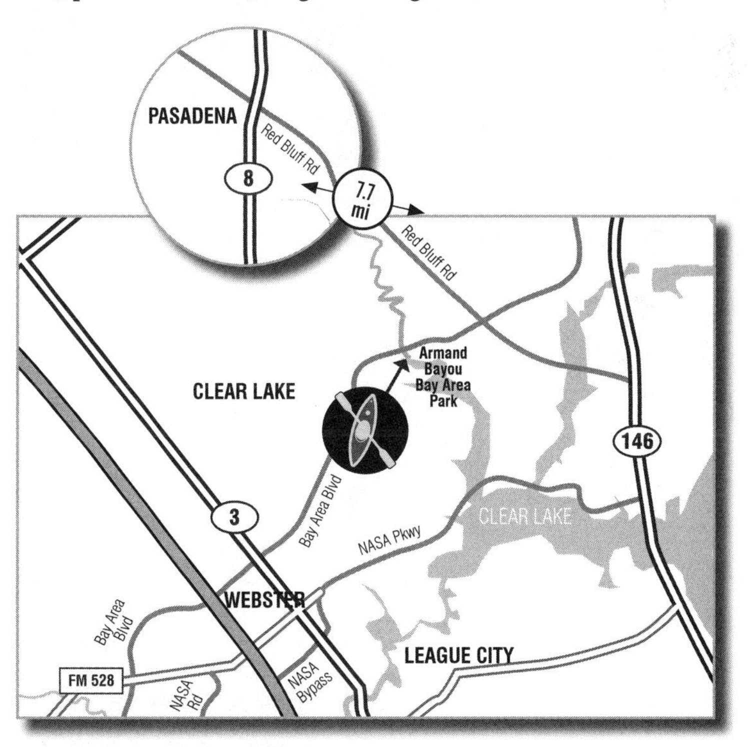

Challenger 7 Park

2301 West NASA Blvd.

N 29 30.388, W 95 07.994 Elevation: 4 feet

FROM THE INTERSECTION of Sam Houston Parkway (Beltway 8) east and I-45 south, continue south on I-45, to FM 528. Turn right on FM 528, .2 miles to the second light. Turn left on W NASA Blvd. and follow the signs into the park. The paved launch is free and open only to canoe and kayak use. This park is on Clear Creek. The creek is well protected on both sides with trees so you

will be able to get shelter from the wind. There are also wetland lakes off the main creek to explore.

There is a fish consumption warning for this body of water. The water flow is slow under normal conditions. The park has public rest rooms. There is also a boardwalk and trail system for jogging and biking. Observation towers for birding, an overlook of the park, BBQ pits and a learning center make this a great spot for everyone even if you do not paddle.

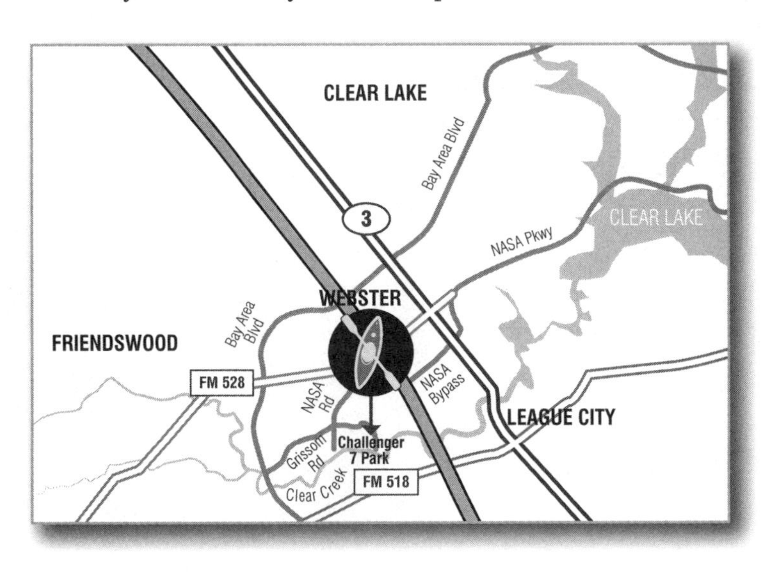

Riverside Inn Marina San Jacinto River

17433 River Road Channelview, TX 77530 (281) 452-0609

N 29 47.914, W 95 04.783 Elevation: 7 feet

FROM THE INTERSECTION of Sam Houston Parkway, (Beltway 8) east and I-10 east, continue on I-10 east toward Beaumont 3.7 miles to exit 785 Magnolia Ave. Turn left and travel .4 miles to River Road. Turn right on river road and travel 1.5 miles to the launch. This is a fee launch, $5.00. The launch

is paved and has nice docks around the site. Plenty of parking is available. New owners have taken over in 2012 and are working to make it even better.

This is the lower end of the San Jacinto River. Expect boat traffic of all kinds. This area is a good, close place to paddle if there is not much wind. Coastal conditions would apply with shallow bays and nowhere to hide from rough weather. This will be a mixture of fresh and salt water. There is a fish consumption advisory on this area of the river.

There are rest rooms available, a grill and a bar on this site. They open at 11 am. I was there early, and the place was clean. I met with one of the new owners, and they are working hard to make this a good place to launch.

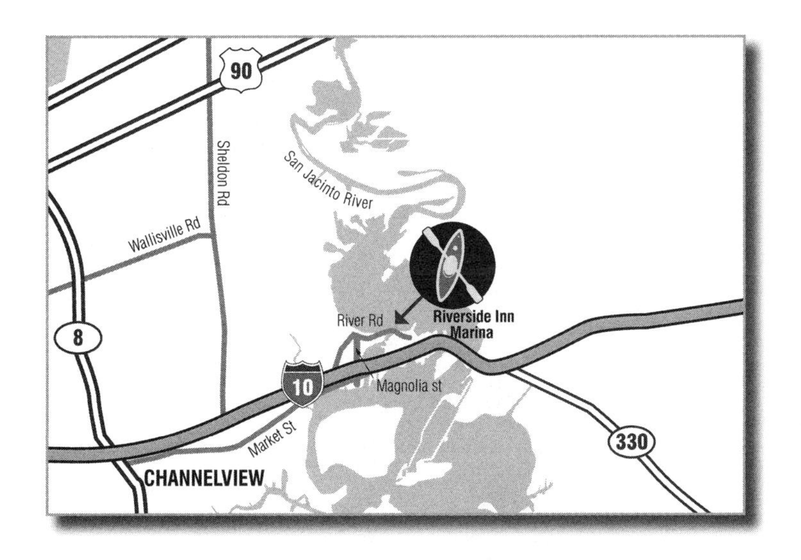

BUFFALO BAYOU

BUFFALO BAYOU BOASTS 10 different launch locations starting from Highway 6 on the west side all the way to downtown. I traveled to each one and found that some were not that accessible. Here is the list.

Hwy 6	22
Memorial Mews	24
Dairy Ashford	26
West Sam Houston Tollway	28
Briar Bend	30
Woodway/Memorial Launch	32
Hogg Bird Sanctuary	34
Eleanor Tinsley	36
Sabine Street	38
Allen's Landing	40

Hwy 6

N 29 46.163, W 95 38.602 Elevation: 68 feet

FROM THE INTERSECTION of I-10 west and Hwy 6 west, travel south on Hwy 6 for 1.1 miles

The parking lot is on the right (west side) and a bit hard to see. The launch is on the opposite side (east) of Hwy 6 from the parking lot on the west side. There is a place to pull off and drop off kayaks but not designat-

ed as a spot to leave your vehicle. Drop off your boats on the east side of Hwy 6.

The launch site is a steep concrete bank. Be very careful when launching from here, the bayou can be swift when water is being discharged from the reservoir. This launch would be recommended as a put-in spot only. Then float down stream to another take-out along Buffalo Bayou. Fishing in Buffalo Bayou can be productive. The bayou supports good numbers of sunfish, bass and catfish. Eating fish from the bayou is not recommended.

No amenities.

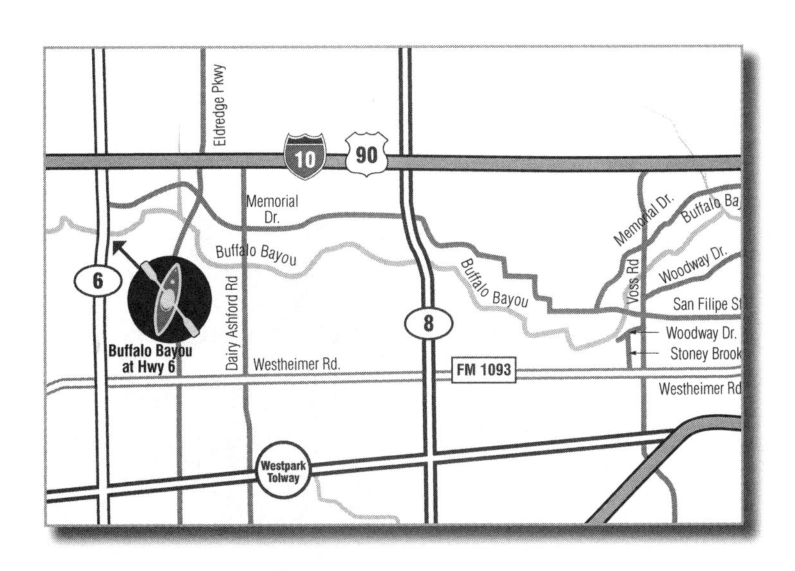

Memorial Mews

N 29 46.400, W 95 37.400 Elevation: 77 feet

FROM THE INTERSECTION of I-10 west and Eldridge turn south on Eldridge, to Memorial drive. Turn right on Memorial drive .5 miles. Mews Park will be on your right.

This launch site is actually on Langham Creek. This creek is a narrow, protected waterway that flows south into Buffalo Bayou. No ramp available. You will need to portage your boat about 200 yards down the bank from the parking lot. You will need to navigate some tree roots and a fairly steep bank into the water.

Langham Creek is narrow and slow in this area. I did not make this paddle but it is .5 miles to paddle down to Buffalo Bayou There are rest rooms available in the park. This is also part of an extensive walking / biking trail system along Buffalo Bayou

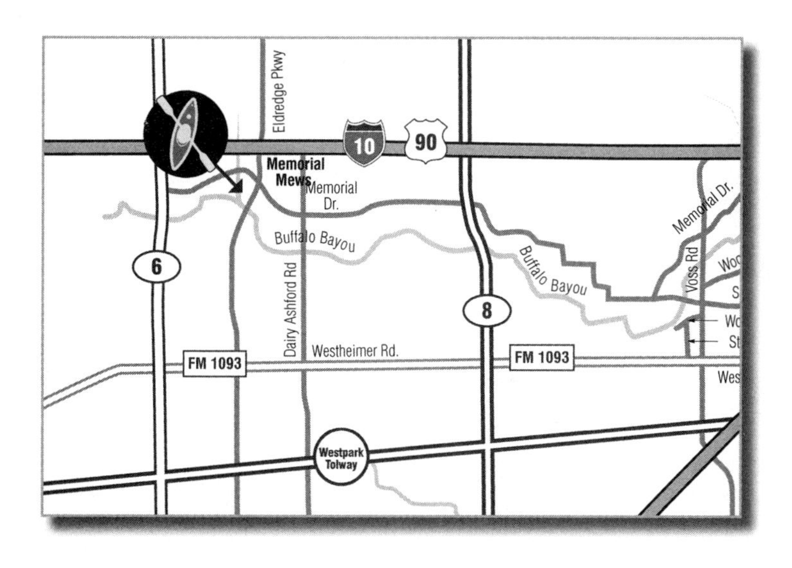

Dairy Ashford Launch

1001 S. Dairy Ashford

N 29 45.700, W 95 36.383 Elevation: 73 feet

From the intersection of I-10 west and Dairy Ashford, travel south 1.1 miles on Dairy Ashford. When you get to the bridge that crosses the bayou, the parking lot will be the next left, next to the office building. The launch is about 200 yards down the bank under the bridge. You will need to portage

from the parking lot down the hill to the water. There are wide wooden steps at the bottom along the water edge to launch from.

The bayou is a bit wider in this area, but still many overhanging trees.

There is plenty of public 24-hour parking available here, but no amenities.

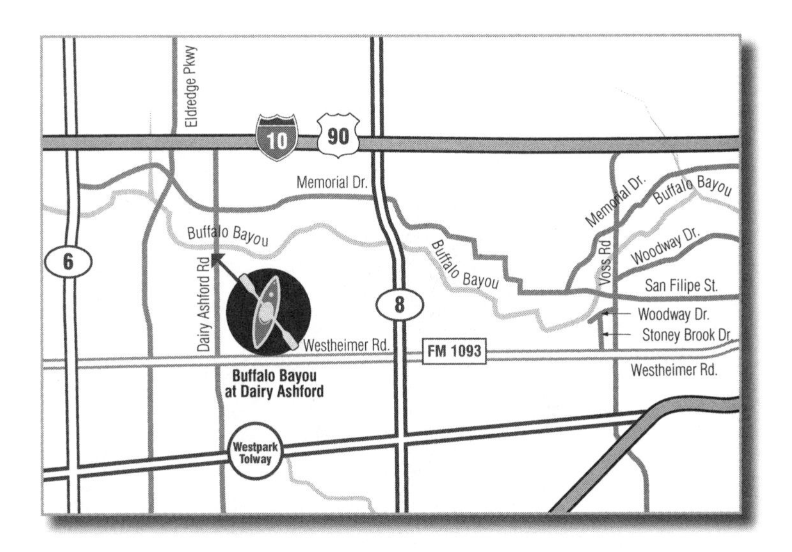

West Sam Houston Tollway Launch

N 29 45.733, W 95 33.500 Elevation: 48 feet

From I-10 and Sam Houston Tollway west, take the frontage road South of I-10, 1.3 miles. The frontage will dead end, and you will have to turn left over the freeway then back right on the east side of the freeway frontage road.

This is a two way street. Continue .3 miles, and the parking lot is on the right. This area is part of

Terry Hershey Park. You will need to portage down a concrete trail about 150 yards to the bayou. This is a popular spot for bike trail riders along the bayou. You will not have much luck going upstream from this point.

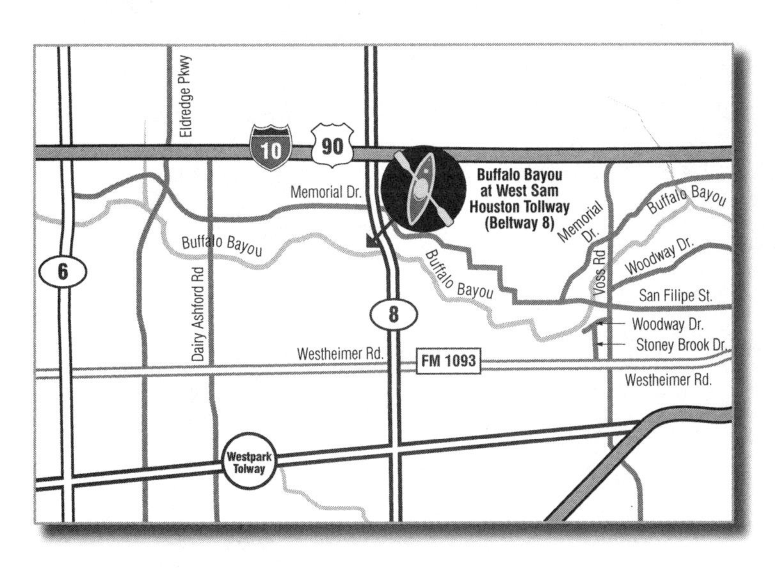

Briar Bend Park Launch

N 29 44.763, W 95 30.429 Elevation: 56 feet

From the intersection of Loop 610 West and Woodway Dr., travel west on Woodway Dr., 2.9 miles to Voss. Turn left on Voss 1.1 miles to Westheimer. Turn right on Westheimer .02 miles to Stoney Brook Drive. Turn right on Stoney Brook Dr., .5 miles to Woodway Dr. Turn left on

Woodway Dr., and Briar Bend Park is on your right. There is street parking only here. The launch ramp is in the back of the park. From the ramp sign go left, down a very steep set of wood and gravel steps.

You will need to portage 50-75 yards down the hill to the bayou. Use caution as this area can be very slippery. Concrete blocks make up the launch site along the bayou edge. The bayou narrows here, and the water is quite swift. Paddling upstream would be difficult.

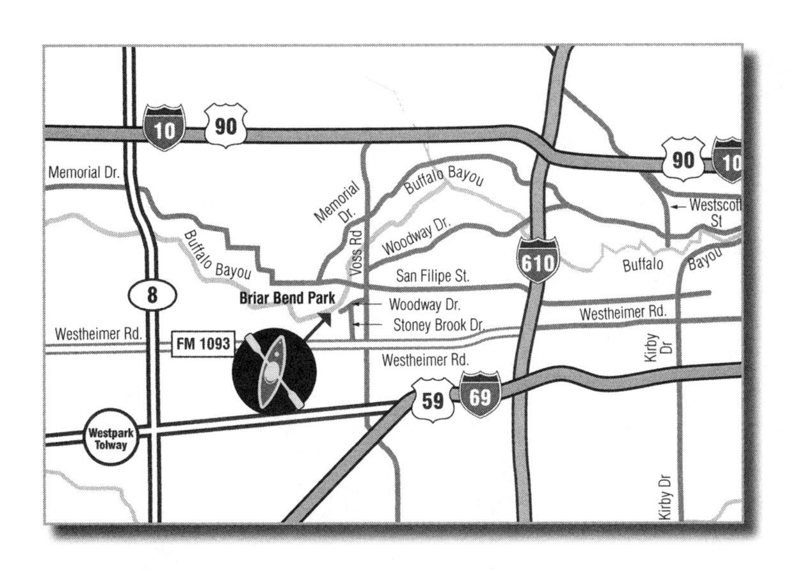

Woodway/Memorial Launch

4700 Woodway

N 29 45.883, W 95 27.417 Elevation: 21 feet

From the intersection of Loop 610 West and Woodway Dr. travel west .1 miles on Woodway. The first light is where N Post Oak intersects with Woodway Dr. The park is on the south side of Woodway Dr. at this intersection. The parking

area is not very large so it is easy to miss if you are not careful. The parking lot was under construction and closed, spring 2014

The launch is west down the hill under the bridge. There is a set of secured timber steps that will assist with entry and exit. The path down to the bayou is pretty clear, but you will need to portage about 200 yards

The bayou is only 15-20 yards wide in this area.

No amenities here but it is close to many of the city offerings.

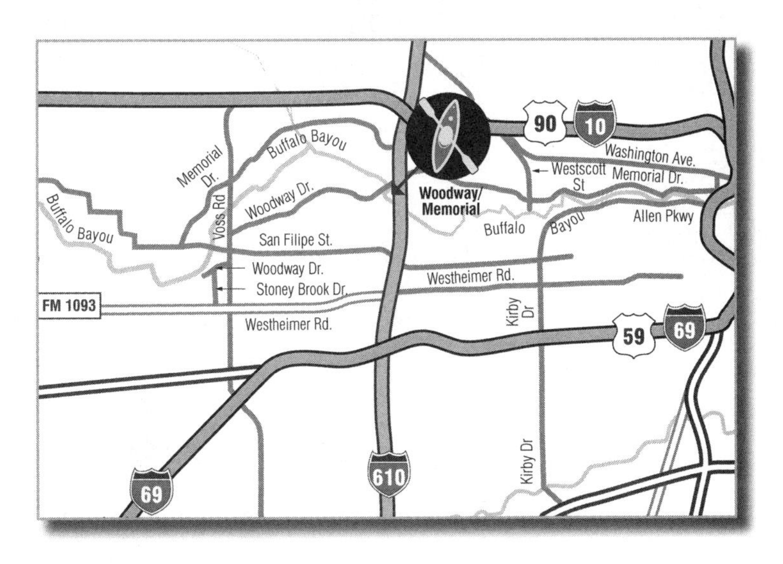

Hogg Bird Sanctuary

100 Westcott St.

N 29 45.500, W 95 25.300 Elevation: 28 feet

FROM THE INTERSECTION of I-10 west and Washington Ave., continue south on Washington Street to Westcott. Stay right and travel south on Westcott across Memorial Dr., 1 mile to the dead end into the park.

There is no maintained launch here. You

would have to bushwhack down to the steep bank of the bayou. It is listed on the Buffalo Bayou Paddle trail, but not really a launch site I could find.

It is a great park, but skip the kayak.

No amenities. Park closes at 5 pm.

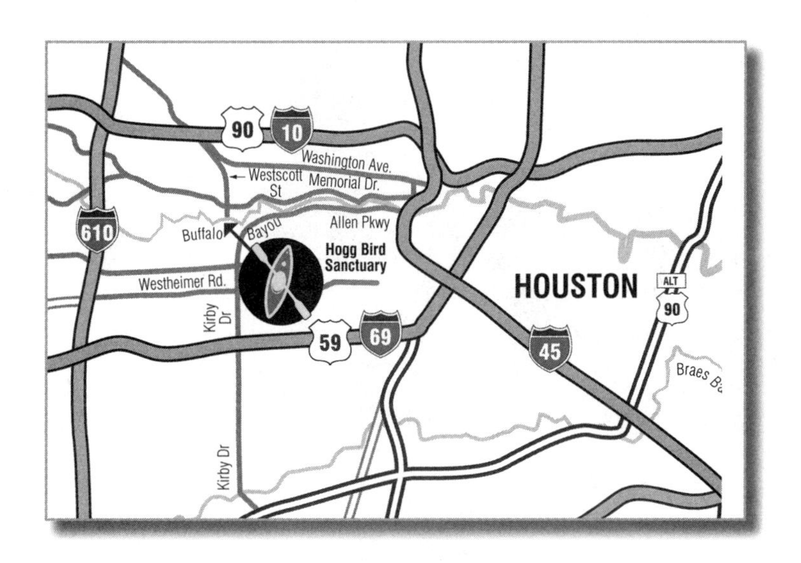

Eleanor Tinsley Park

500 Allen Parkway

N 29 45.700, W 95 22.700 Elevation: 34 feet

FROM THE INTERSECTION of I-10 west and I-45, take I-45 south and exit, Allen Parkway. Eleanor Tinsley Park runs along the north side of Allen Parkway. There are several parking areas along Allen Parkway. The best spot to launch is from below the Police Depart-

ment Memorial. There is a nice sandy bank to put in or take out This area of the park was under construction in the fall of 2013 so look for changes and upgrades.

No amenities here.

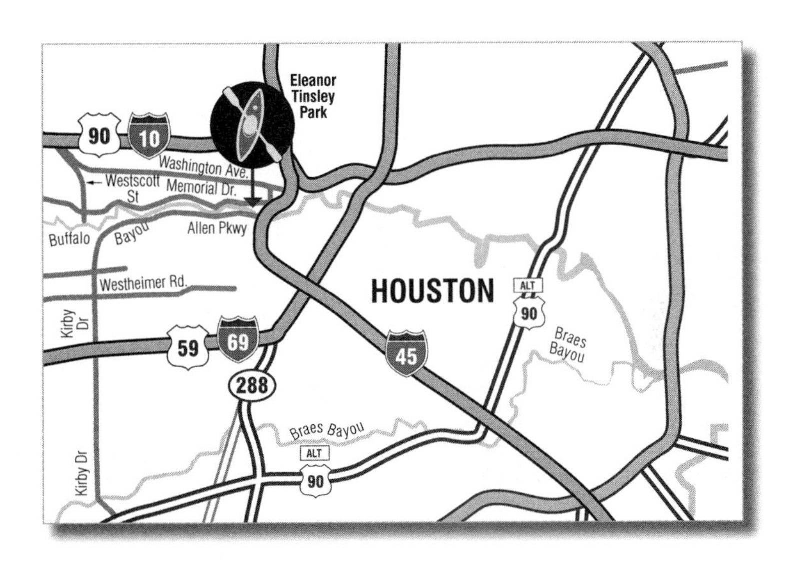

Sabine Street Launch

200 Sabine Street

N 29 45.733, W 95 22.417 **Elevation: 14 feet**

From the intersection of I-10 west and Washington Ave. turn south on Washington Ave, 3.1 miles to Sawyer St. and turn right. Continue 1 mile on Sawyer, to Sabine St. Turn right on Sabine, travel 2 blocks. The stairs down to the launch will be just before the intersection with Allen Parkway.

Parking close is an issue. There is street parking along Sabine St., but it fills up fast. The launch is across from the Lee and Joe

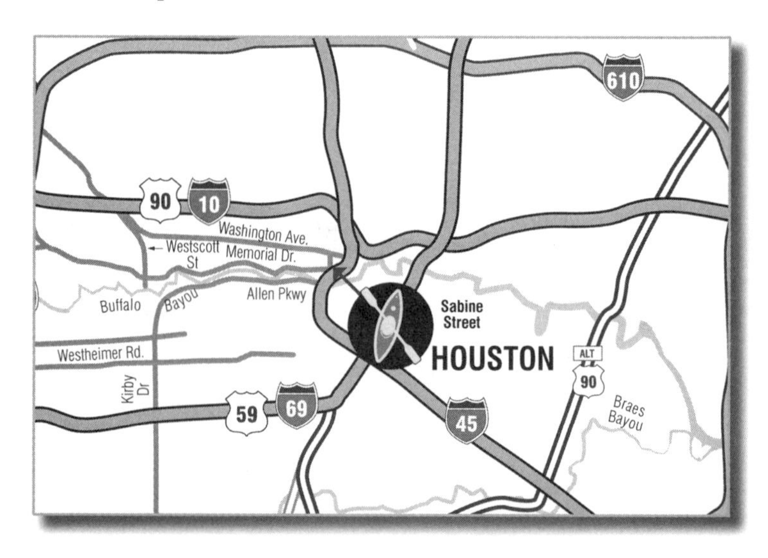

Jamail skate park. You will need to portage two flights of stairs to get to the bayou. The launch is concrete and has rings where you can secure your boat. From here you can paddle up stream to Eleanor Tinsley Park or downstream to Allen's landing. There is restricted water space on the bayou south of Allen's Landing.

Allen's Landing

510 Preston Ave.

N 29 45.883, W 95 21.550 Elevation: 14 feet

From the intersection of I-10 west and Washington Ave., take Washington south 3.5 miles. Preston Street will Y off to the right just past Houston Ave., stay to the right and travel .5 miles to 510 Preston. Only street parking is available.

This launch is in the heart of downtown Houston. You will get a

view from the water that not many see. The launch is concrete. You will need to portage down to the bayou about 200 yards.

Recommended to paddle upstream from here or use as a take-out point. Travel is restricted in the bayou downstream from this launch.

Buffalo Bayou is a semi-natural stream with flow and water quality conditions that are constantly influenced by many factors. Releases from Addicks and Barker Reservoirs, storm water runoff, discharge from sewage treatment plants, and natural springs all affect this waterway.

Kayaking should not be attempted in high and turbulent water conditions. Log jams, known as "strainers", can be very hazardous, and should be avoided; always portage around them.

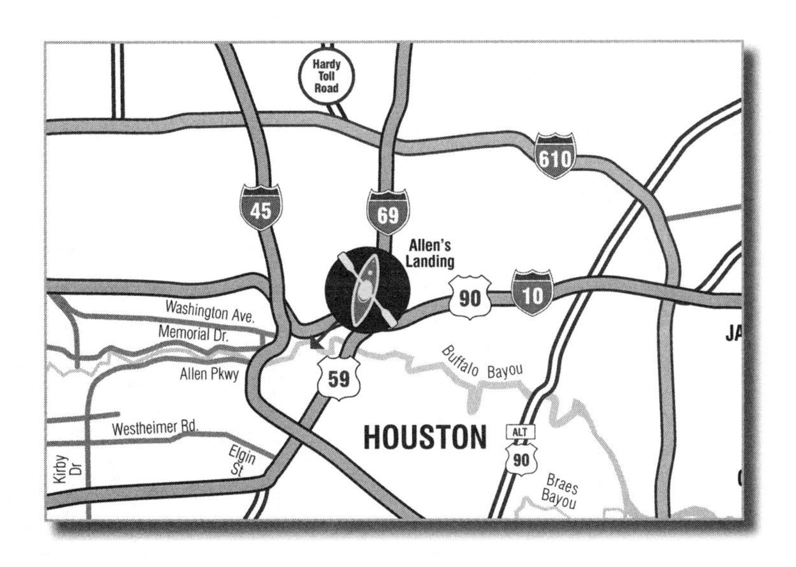

HOUSTON EAST

THESE LAUNCHES ARE to be considered more brackish water than true freshwater destinations. They are included as freshwater but you may very well be fishing speckled trout and redfish.

McCullum Park 44

Hugo Park 46

Gou Hole 48

Trinity River Island/Wallisville Lake Project 50

Trinity River at I-10 W (East and West) 52

River Terrace Park 54

McCullum Park

N 29 44.687, W 94 49.690 Elevation: 20 feet

From the intersection of I 10 east and Sam Houston Toll Way (Beltway 8), continue east on I-10, 22 miles to FM 565. Turn right and travel 3.7 miles, and turn left on FM 3180. In 1.9 miles FM 3180 turns into FM 2354. Continue on 2354, and travel a total of 3.7 miles south. Turn left on McCullum Park Road (street sign). Travel 1.4 miles to the park. This is a free launch site, but it does have

its challenges. You have to park and unload at the top of a big hill, then drive your vehicle out away from the water and park several hundred yards outside the fenced park. The road down to the water is steep and very rocky. The launch is off the shoreline about 100 yards left from this road. There is no way to get close to this launch with a vehicle. If you have a cart you will need it for this launch site. If you don't have a cart, you will have to carry your boat or drag it to the launch.

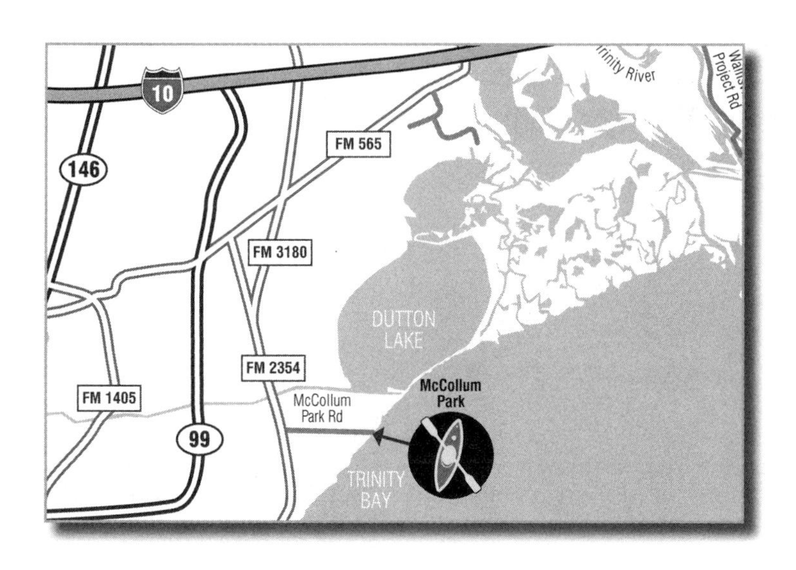

Hugo Park

1705 Gou Hole Rd.. Cove, Texas

N 29 48.732, W 94 47.730 Elevation: 11 feet

From the intersection of I-10 east and Sam Houston Toll Way (Beltway 8), continue east on I-10, 22 miles to FM 565. Turn right and travel .7 miles to GOU Hole Rd. Turn left and travel 1.6 miles to a Y in the road. Bear left and go 1 mile to Hugo Park.

This is a very well maintained free launch with two

fairly new paved launches and a floating dock. There is plenty of paved parking and room to maneuver around. Coastal conditions apply here, with open water and little shelter. Wind would be a factor. Paddle back to the north to I-10 and across the river to marsh for more cover. This launch has rest rooms but no other facilities. Take care of your last minute needs before you leave I-10 exit.

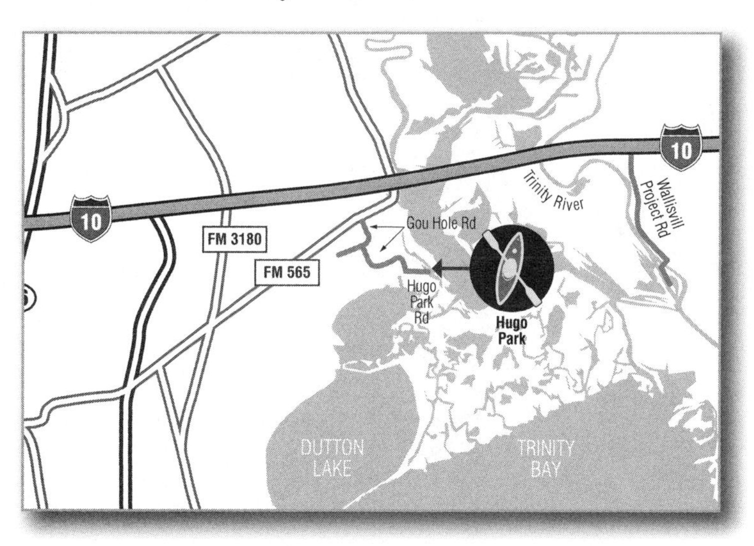

Gou Hole

N 29 48.595, W 94 48.103 Elevation: 5 feet

From the intersection of I-10 east and Sam Houston Toll Way (Beltway 8), continue east on I-10 22 miles to FM 565. Turn right and travel .7 miles to GOU Hole Rd. Turn left and travel 1.6 miles to a Y in the road. Bear right to go .5 miles through the neighborhood to Gou Hole Launch.

This is an older launch with two small ramps and lots of gravel parking. You launch into a

slough that feeds out into the Old and Lost River system.

This launch is only about .5 miles south of the Hugo Park launch. It is on my short list of places to get my boat wet soon. Wind would be a factor. Paddle back to the north to I-10 and across the river to marsh and more cover. Shallow water conditions can be a problem at this launch. If the water is too low you will end up stuck on the mud flats. Use caution.

The Old and Lost rivers interconnect with the Trinity River along this section south of I-10. Fishing prospects are very good for multiple species.

No amenities.

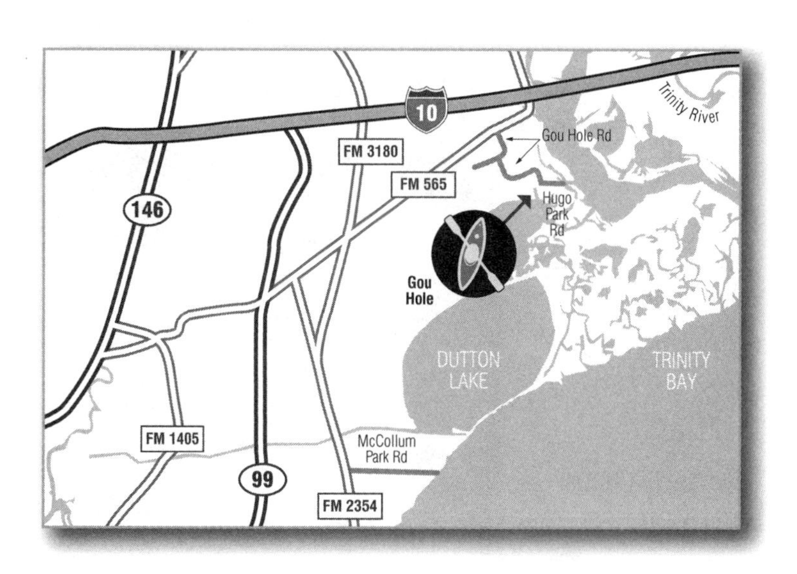

Trinity River Island/Wallisville Lake Project

N 29 48.503, W 94 43.781 Elevation: 7 feet

FROM THE INTERSECTION of I-10 east and Sam Houston Toll Way (Beltway 8), continue east on I-10 from Beltway 8, 25.4 miles and take exit 807. Travel just to the end of the ramp, and turn right into the Trinity River Island Recreation Area. Continue 1.8 miles down to the visitor center. The boat ramp is behind the visitor center

This is a free launch and very well maintained.

Two paved launches and docks attached. There is plenty of parking in a gravel lot. There is an extended roadway to allow for easy turning and backing into the ramp. The river is fairly well protected from the wind in this section. Water conditions will vary with water flow conditions. Always consider runoff and other factors that will have an effect on the river. Rest rooms are located inside the visitor center. This center has several very educational exhibits and also additional rest rooms out close to the ramp. There is also a very nice elevated bird observation platform located here.

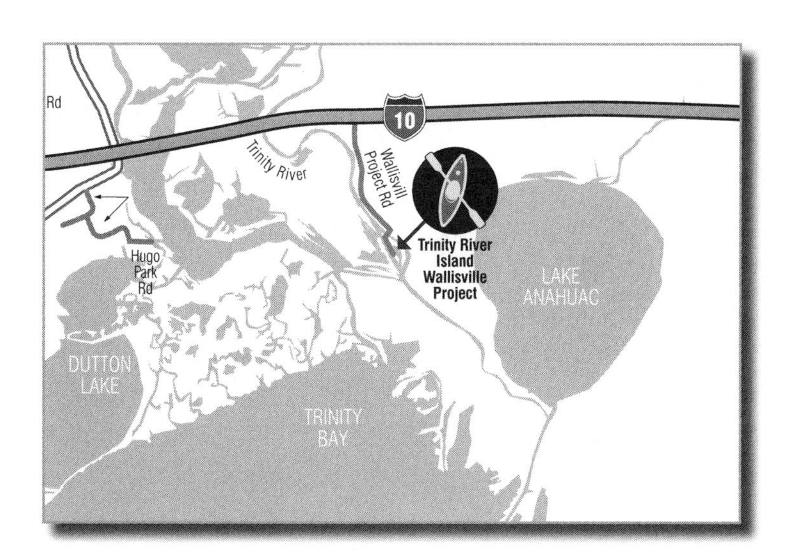

Trinity River at I-10 West; East and West

East: N 29 50.240, W 94 45.768 Elevation: East 6 feet
West: N 29 50.198, W 94 45.878 Elevation: West 2 feet

THERE ARE TWO launch points here, one on each side of the bridge.

From the intersection of I-10 east and Sam Houston Toll Way (Beltway 8), continue east on I-10, 24.4 miles. To launch on the west side, take Exit 805. This is a turn around with the launch under the bridge on the west side of the river.

To launch on the east side of the river continue over the bridge to Exit 807. Exit right and continue to the first intersection, Wallisville-Liberty road. U-turn under the freeway and continue along the feeder, back westbound to the launch point under the bridge on the east side of the river. The east and west

ramps are free launch points. The west site has one lane and is paved. It is a bit grown up and could use some cleaning up. The east side is just a sand beach but is acceptable to launch a kayak.

The Trinity is not very wide at this point and there were two jet skis launching with wave boards, the day I was there. This section does seem to be very busy.

The river is fairly well-protected from the wind in this section. Water conditions will vary with water flow conditions. Always consider river conditions, rainfall, and other factors that will have an effect on the river.

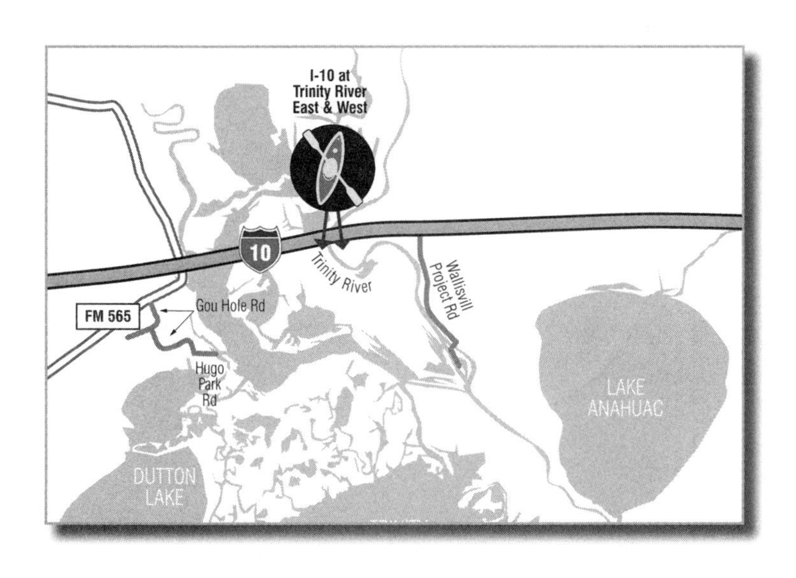

River Terrace Park

N 29 46.903, W 95 06.059 Elevation: 13 feet

From the intersection of I-10 east and Sam Houston Parkway east (Beltway 8), continue east on I-10, 3 miles to Cedar/Bayou exit. Exit and turn right on Bayou Dr. Travel .1 miles to Market Street and turn right. The park is immediately on your left.

This is a free launch with a paved ramp that will accommodate two vehicles. This area of the river system has a lot of big boat traffic. There were tugs and barges parked right across from the launch. It may be a place for a short paddle, but use extreme caution. These tug combinations push a lot of water, and you are no match for them in a kayak.

There is a fish consumption advisory on this area of the river. Coastal Conditions apply here. There is so much traffic here that the water will be muddy most of the time. Rest rooms and playground equipment are also available here.

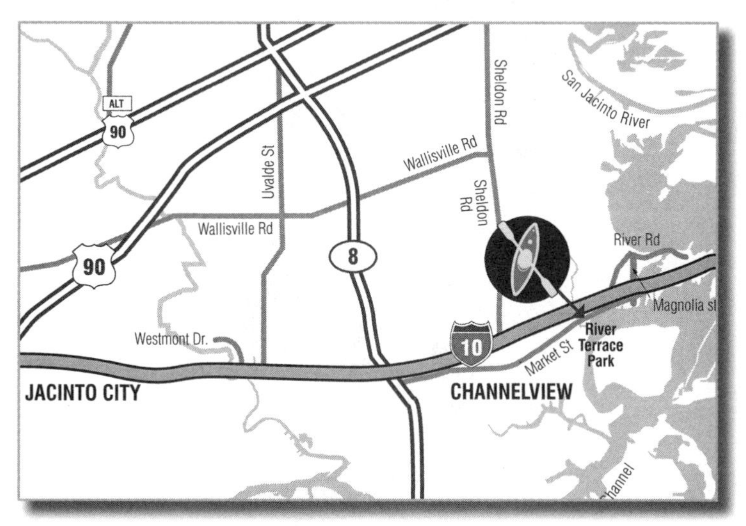

LAKE HOUSTON

ON LAKE HOUSTON we mapped three different locations with a total of five launch sites.

Luce Bayou, Ponderosa Ramp 58

BJ's Marina 60

Alexander Deussen Park 62

Luce Bayou, Ponderosa Ramp

N 30 03.384, W 95 05.959 Elevation: 42 feet

Hwy 59 north to New Caney. Exit FM 1485 turn right. .1 miles turn right on loop 494. .2 miles turn left on 1485. Continue 10.9 miles and turn right on Huffman-Cleveland Rd. Follow 2.6 miles to Ponderosa boat ramp.

This is a fee ramp. At the time I was there it was $7. I will say there are other places you can slip a boat in along the bayou, but for me this access is worth it. The launch is paved and clean, safe, and has plenty of parking. It will put you in the bayou about mid-way between 1485 and Lake Houston. The fees are collected on the honor system. Power boats are plentiful on the weekends, but tend to mainly use the southern section closer to the lake. This is a favorite spot of mine and is very kayak friendly. If you like a calm paddle, go north away from the lake. There are many coves and lily pad sections along both banks. There are plenty of coves and places where you can get out of the main channel. It is not a long paddle to get to the main body of Lake Houston. The flow on this bayou is very slow, so it is always a nice, flat stretch of water. It is also very protected from winds, so it is a good choice most anytime.

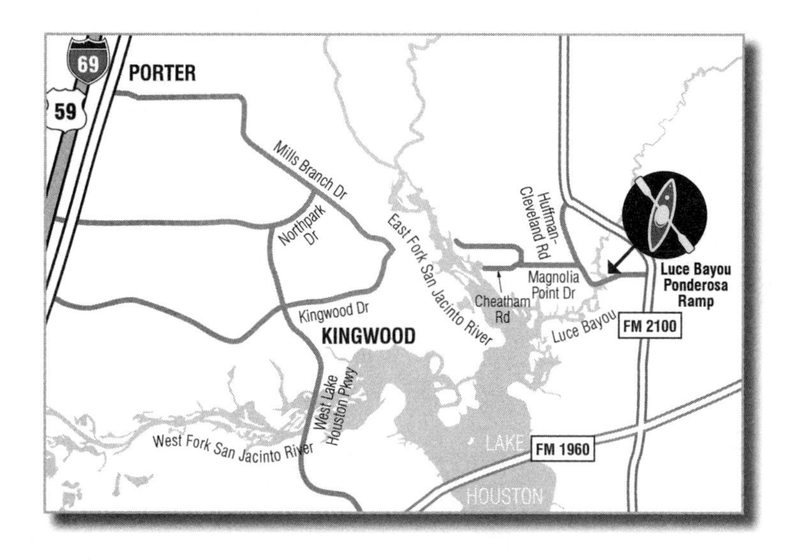

BJ's Marina

2907 Calvin Road Huffman, Texas

N 30 03.547, W 95 07.907 **Elevation: 53 feet**

TRAVEL HWY 59 north of Houston to New Caney. Exit FM 1485 and turn right. .1 miles turn right on loop 494. .2 miles turn left on 1485. Continue 10.9 miles and turn right on Huffman Cleveland Rd. Travel 1.2 miles to Magnolia Point Dr. Turn right, travel 1.1 miles, and stay to the left on Cheatham Rd. It will

dead end into BJ's Marina. One paved launch here. $5 fee to launch your boat. This marina is on the northeast side of Lake Houston. It is somewhat protected and provides a nice place to paddle. If you travel upstream, you will end up at the lower end of Lake Houston Park. This is the confluence of Peach Creek and the East Fork of the San Jacinto River. The marina office is not open every day, so a drop box is used to pay launch fee. Restrooms and the store are available on weekends.

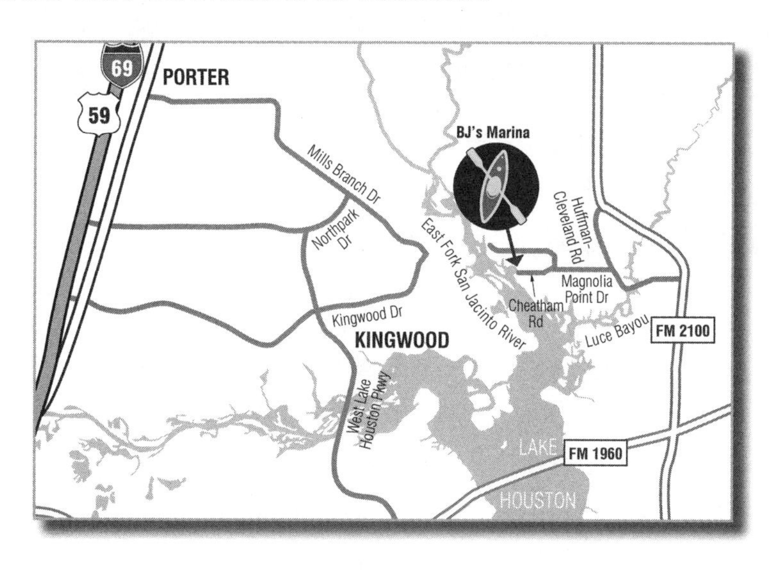

Alexander Deussen Park

12303 Sonnier Street, Houston

N 29 55.101, W 95 09.013 **Elevation: 51 feet**

THIS IS A 309-acre county park on the west side of Lake Houston. Very well-maintained and includes three, free boat launch ramps. From the intersection of Beltway 8 East and Lake Houston Parkway, take Lake Houston Parkway east 3.1 miles. The park entrance is on the right.

The three boat ramps are all paved. The middle ramp can accommodate at least two vehicles at a time The ramp on the very north side of the park is smaller and situated on a protected slough. This area would be my first choice to launch a kayak.

This is a popular park and can be busy on the weekends. If

you want to fish the lower section of the lake and dam area this is the spot to launch from.

This park is very well-maintained and has several pavilions and multiple handicap accessible restroom facilities. The park has a playground, hike and bike trails, a wildlife exhibit and jogging trails.

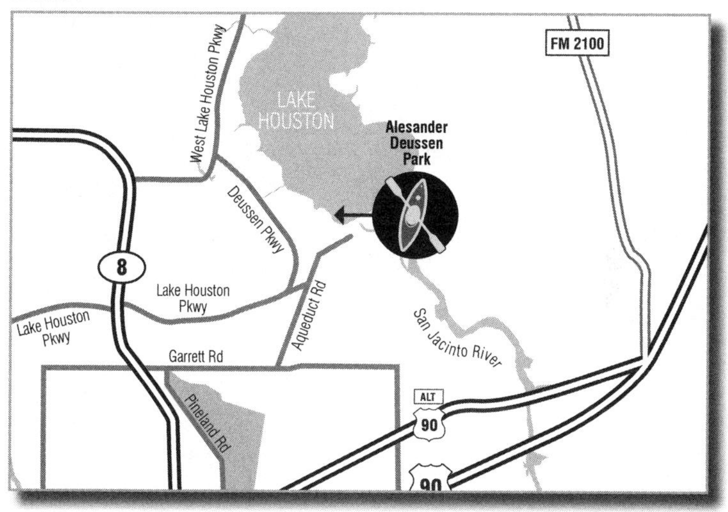

• • •

Lake Houston is 11,854 acres, created in 1954 for Houston city water supply. You will have plenty of room to explore. Deussen Park is on the far south end of the lake so try the west shoreline and along the dam. As with most any lake near a large metropolitan area, you will have to contend with some power boat traffic. At Luce Bayou, the water is stained to clear and has a reasonable flow most of the time. It boasts 35 miles of navigable waters Do not attempt to travel in flood conditions. The Ponderosa web site has a link to the USGS water gage height and flow.

The water at BJ's Marina, under normal flow should be slow enough to make this a nice protected paddle area. The water will be stained to muddy depending on rainfall and other conditions affecting water flow. Bank access is also available under the FM 1960 bridge. This lake and all these launches are quickly affected by any rain.

Paddling on an open lake brings wind and other weather factors into consideration. Lake Houston is relatively shallow and at times can appear pretty muddy. The launch points on the north side of the lake are more protected.

Largemouth bass, crappie, and panfish are plentiful. The catfishing is excellent. The drought in 2011 caused the lake to be very low, but by the time of this writing, water levels were back to normal. Fishing around docks and other structure should produce satisfactory results.

LAKE WOODLANDS

ONE LAUNCH SITE is profiled on Lake Woodlands, situated in the vibrant, picturesque community of The Woodlands, 25 miles north of downtown Houston.

North Shore Park 66

North Shore Park

2505 Lake Woodlands Drive

N 30 10.133, W 95 28.532 Elevation: 129 feet

From the intersection of I-45 north and Sam Houston Parkway north (beltway 8), continue on I-45 north to the Lake Woodlands Dr. exit. Turn left over the freeway (west) 1.8 miles. The park with boat ramp is on the left.

This is a free public boat launch; it is only open from dawn to dusk. Don't get caught too late or they will lock your vehicle in for the night. There is a paved launch and also plenty of bank space to launch from.

This is a shallow lake but it offers a nice paddle. Go north from the launch to have a more nature-friendly paddle. The lake is fairly open so wind can be a factor. No gas motors can be

used. Boats with gas motors are allowed, but only electric motors may be used. Rowing clubs also use this lake for practice so you may have company. Largemouth bass, catfish and bluegill are all present. The water is stained, and fairly shallow throughout the lake. Rest rooms are available.

This is very close to many other attractions in the Woodlands.

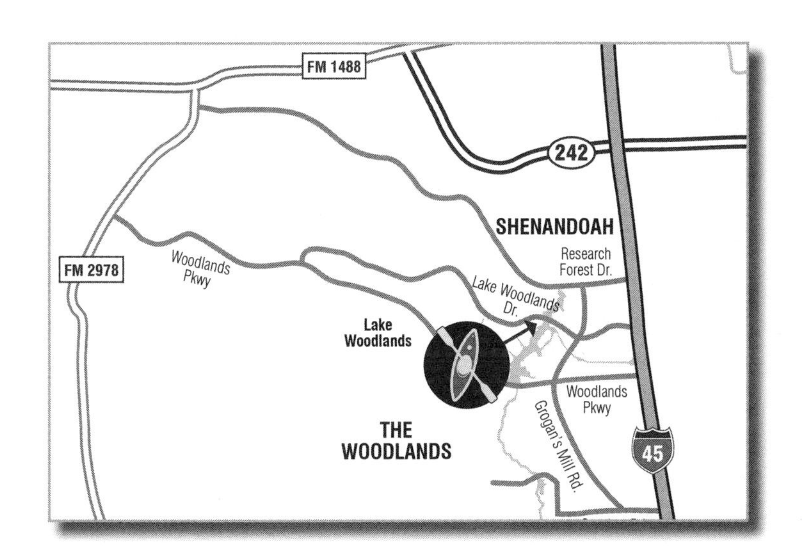

LAKE CONROE

LAKE CONROE IS primarily open water in the lower two-thirds of the reservoir, with some standing timber still present along the river channel in the upper reaches. Most of the standing timber is slightly submerged when the lake is at conservation pool, making navigation hazardous for power boats in these areas.

Cagle and Stubblefield are both located on the upper reaches, or northern end of the lake.

FM 830 Ramp 70

Cagle Launch 72

Stubblefield Ramp 74

Scott's Ridge 76

FM 830 Ramp

N 30 24.791, W 95 34.291 Elevation: 227 feet

From the intersection of I-45 and FM 830, north of Conroe, Texas, travel west on FM 830, 5.5 miles, FM 830 will dead end into the ramp.

This is one of a very few free boat ramps on Lake Conroe. It will be busy most days. It has two paved launches and a very nice sandy beach area off to the right of the ramps, perfect for kayak launching. Lake Conroe has a surface area of just over 20,000 acres. Most of the shoreline has been developed and lots of power boat and PWC (jet ski) traffic is to be expected. From the 830 ramp it is a nice paddle north to the 1097 bridge. As with any open water, wind can be an issue. Fluctuations in depth can be severe in the lake, depending on water usage and rainfall.

No amenities are available at this site.

Remember that parking may also be an issue on busy weekends.

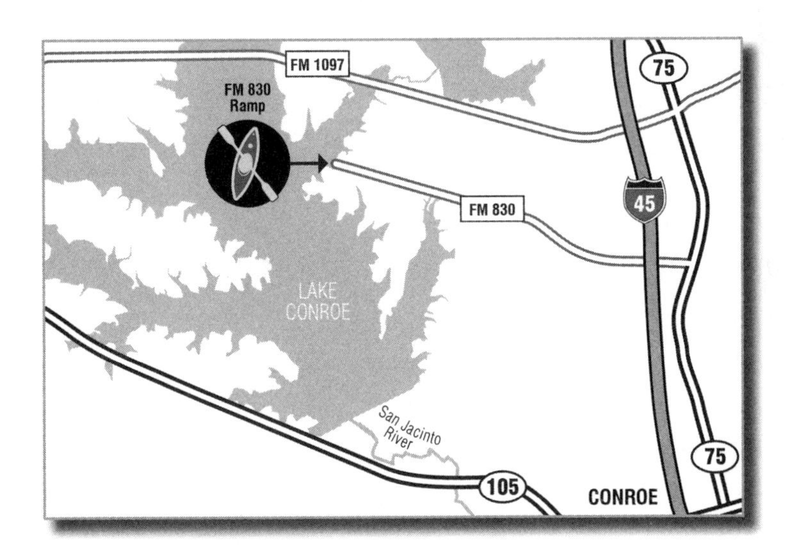

Cagle Launch

N 30 31.130, W 95 35.495 **Elevation: 211 feet**

From the intersection of, I-45 north and FM 1375 in New Waverly, Texas, travel west on FM 1375, 5.8 miles. Turn left and continue to the boat ramp. This ramp is maintained by the National Forest Service and has very visible signs.

The recreation area has a day use fee of $5.

There is a nice

paved two-lane ramp and a floating dock. Camping is also available at this site.

Restrooms and showers are available here as well. There is plenty of paved parking.

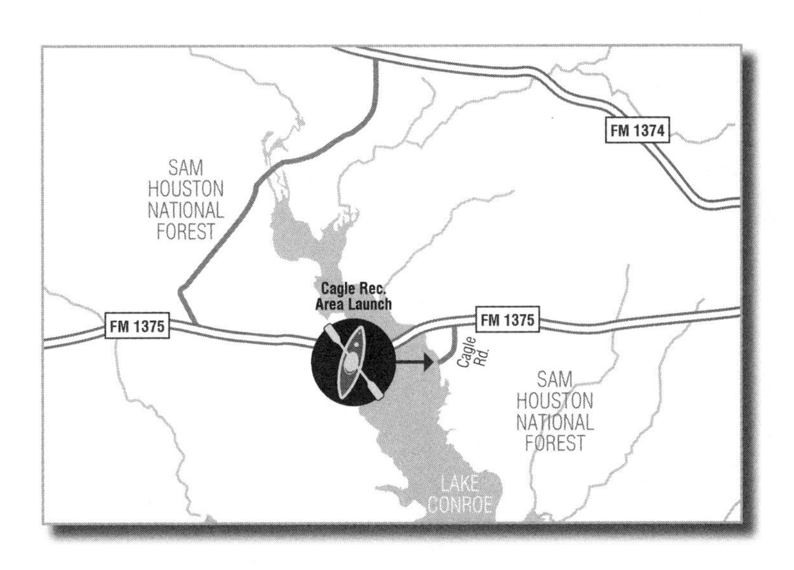

Stubblefield Ramp

N 30 33.833, W 95 38.154 Elevation: 234 feet

FROM THE INTERSECTION of I-45 north and FM 1375 in New Waverly, Texas, continue west on FM 1375, 9.8 miles. Turn right on Stubblefield Lake Rd., and travel 3.4 miles, on the paved road to the ramp.

This is a free launch site. There is a gravel, one-lane ramp, and it is located on the east side of the bridge. This is a

popular fishing place for folks who like to bank fish as well. Parking is available on both sides of the road near the ramp.

There is a campground located just before you get to the boat ramp. This is a fee area, and camping fees apply. The only rest rooms available are located within the campground.

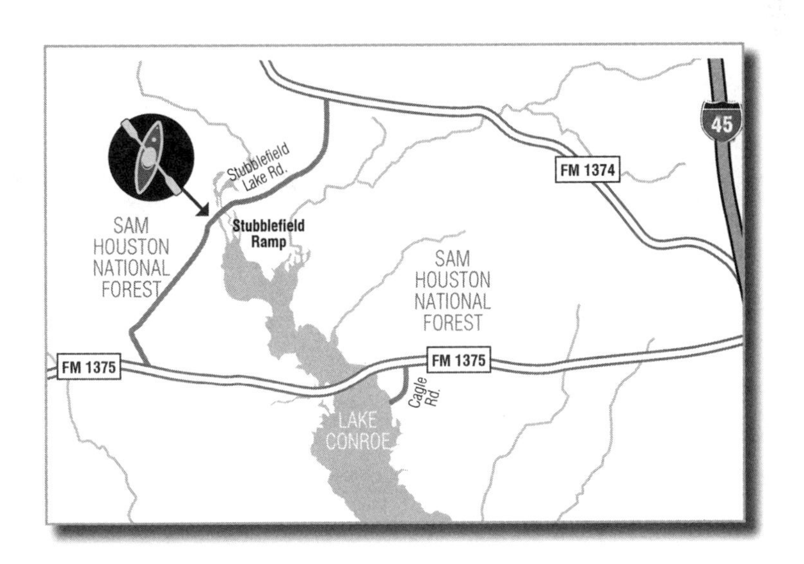

Scott's Ridge

N 30 27.212, W 95 37.802 Elevation: 205 feet

From I-45 north and FM 1097 in Willis, Texas, travel west on FM 1097, 8.5 miles to Scott's Ridge Rd. Turn right and continue to the ramp.

This is a fee ramp, $5 per day for use.

Facility includes a paved boat ramp, restrooms and plenty of paved parking. The area has space for bank fishing as well.

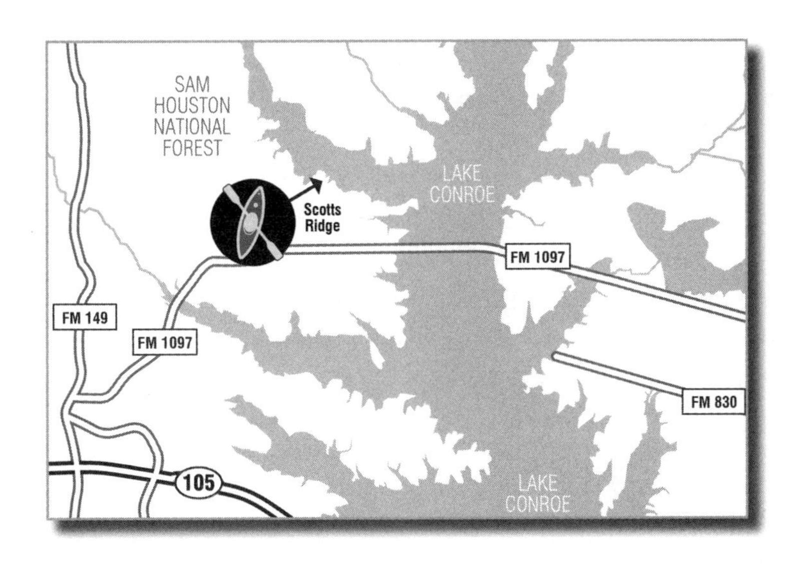

• • •

THERE ARE ALSO several privately operated marinas on Lake Conroe. They are designed for power boats but offer fee-based launch sites:

Stowaway Marina	**I-45 and Calvary Road**
Lochness Marina	**I-45 and Calvary Road**
North Shore Marina	**FM 1097 Bridge**
April Plaza Marina	**Hwy 105**
Inland Marina	**Hwy 105**
Lakeview Marina	**Hwy 105**

Bass and catfish are both popular target fish for anglers on Lake Conroe.

Bass have been regularly stocked into the lake. The standing lake record bass was caught in 2009, and weighed 15.93 pounds.

White and hybrid bass are also favorite targets of many fisherman. Catfish and pan fish round out the list of major species you will find here.

Some man-made structures have been used to create four fish "reefs" in this reservoir. The reefs were placed by TPWD in cooperation with the Seven Coves Bass Club, San Jacinto River Authority and other partners. Anglers may use GPS in conjunction with a fish finder to locate these reefs. The locations can be found through TPWD web site.

LAKE RAVEN

THIS LAKE COVERS 205 acres and was impounded before 1940. One launch site is profiled here.

Huntsville State Park 80

Huntsville State Park

Park Road 40, Huntsville, Texas

N 30 36.860, W 95 32.116 Elevation: 298 feet

From Conroe, Texas continue 23 miles north on I-45 to the Huntsville State Park exit. Exit right, and turn left three miles into the park. The lake has a two-vehicle boat ramp with easy launching. A $5 per person, daily fee is required to enter the state park. In 2013, Lake Raven was named in the top 10 lakes for quality bass over 18 inches.

It is regularly

stocked by TPWD. In 2013, 12,400 Florida bass fingerlings were stocked. In 2010, 2,375 ShareLunker fingerlings were stocked. The lake supports a good population of channel and blue catfish. The state park has well-maintained restrooms. Canoes and paddle boats are available for rent.

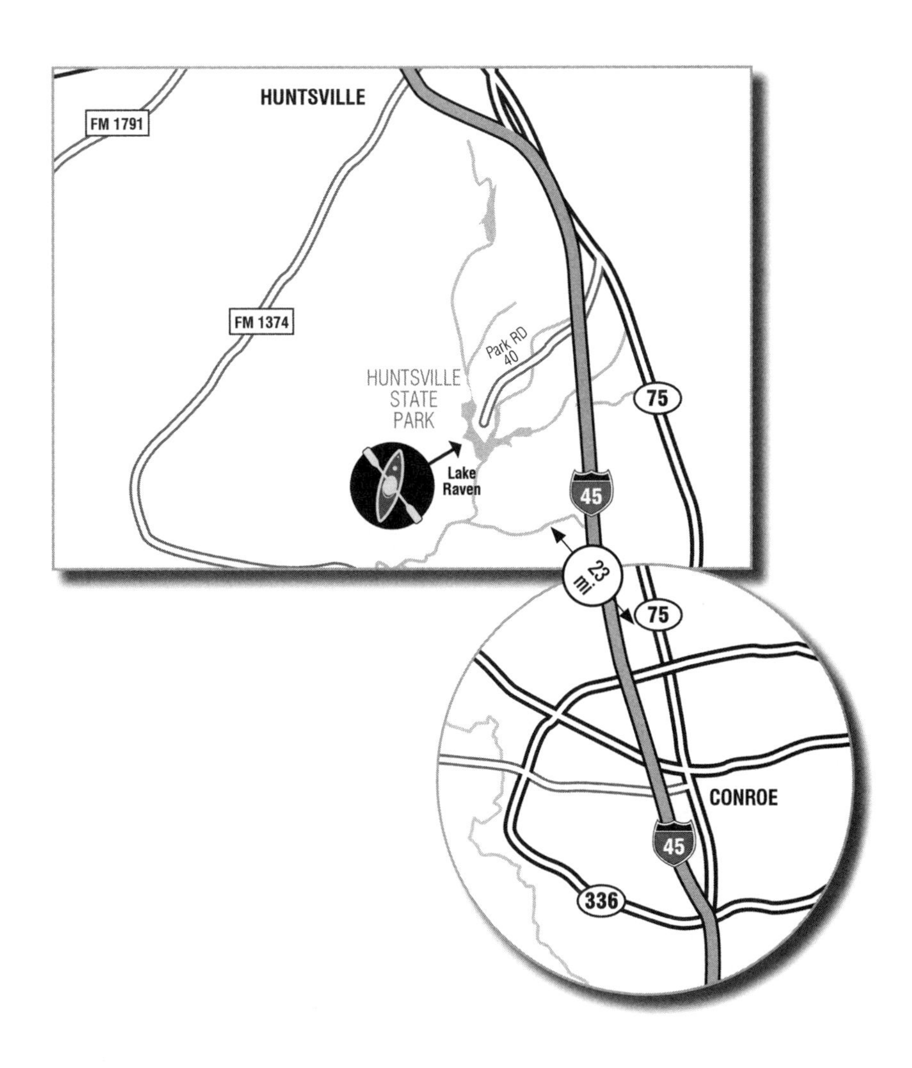

KURTH LAKE

THIS LAKE, LOCATED just above Lake Sam Rayburn, is 726 surface acres and was impounded in 1950. It has 15 miles of shoreline, and a mean depth of 15 feet.

One launch site is profiled.

Kurth Lake Launch 84

Kurth Lake

1300 Rivercrest Drive Lufkin, Texas (closest road for GPS)

N 31 27.061, W 94 42.395 Elevation: 219 feet

Travel Highway 59 north from Houston to Lufkin, Texas. Continue five miles north of Lufkin on Hwy 59 and turn right on Rivercrest drive. Drive 2.2 miles and turn left on Kurth Lake Road. There is a nice big sign here. From Rivercrest to the lake, the roads are narrow and kind of bumpy. This is a

pay to launch site. The minimum is a 3-day permit for $15. You get this from the caretaker on-site (936) 639-4840. There is also a yearly pass available from the City of Lufkin. The launch is a one-boat ramp that is paved. Parking is not paved. This lake is just the right size for kayaking. This was my first trip to this lake, and I can assure you it will not be my last. Plenty of wooded shoreline, so no matter if you have a windy day, you can get to a protected spot. The north end of the lake has a dam. For me the $15 was well spent. The largemouth bass are abundant in this lake. Each year from 2008-2012 over 70,000 Florida bass fingerlings have been stocked into this lake. There are also crappie and catfish as well as bluegill. The bass are the big draw here, though. Lots of hydrilla, lily pads and submerged timber make for the perfect habitat for big bass.

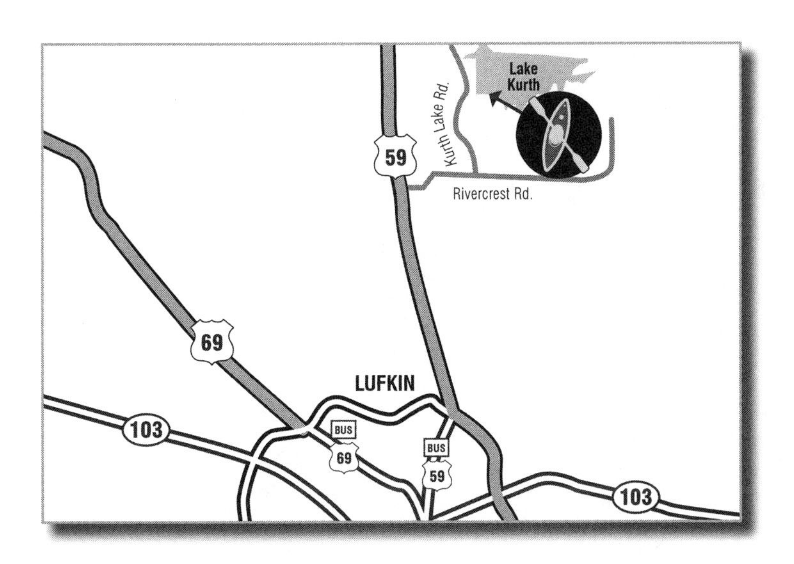

TRINITY RIVER NORTH

THREE LAUNCH SITES are profiled in the area situated along the Trinity River, above and below Lake Livingston.

Trinity River on Highway 59 88

Riverside 90

Harmon Creek Marina 92

Trinity River on Highway 59

N 30 34.191, W 94 56.989   Elevation: 85 feet

FROM THE INTERSECTION of Sam Houston Parkway north and Hwy 59 north, continue north on Hwy 59, 48.7 miles just north of Shepherd, Texas. Turn left across the freeway and continue under the bridge to the ramp.

This is a free, paved, three-lane ramp. It is very long and steep going down to the Trinity River. There is plenty of paved parking available.

The Trinity River has very steep banks and lots of structure. Rip-rap and other rough structure are all along the banks. Always be sure to check the river condition before you plan a trip. It can vary from a flat calm paddle to turbulent, raging, whitewater flood. Remember there are not many available take-out spots along the river so be sure you have a game plan for where to put in and take out.

If that is the same place, understand your paddle capabilities and plan your trip accordingly.

No Restrooms and no other facilities are available at this launch.

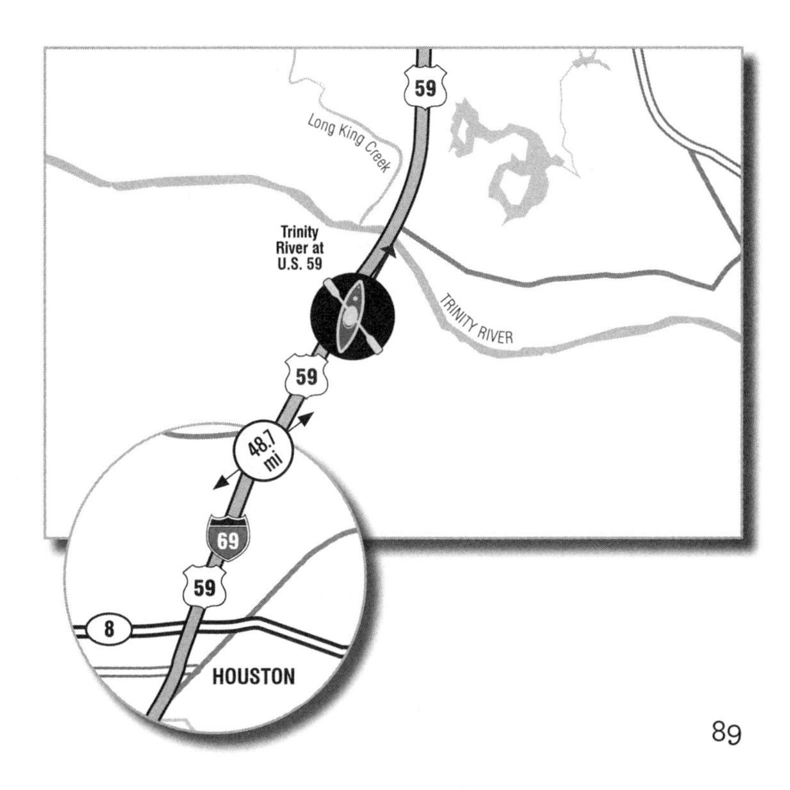

Riverside

N 30 51.514, W 95 23.926 Elevation: 168 feet

FROM I-45 IN Huntsville, take Hwy 19 north 13.5 miles. The public ramp is on the right before you cross the river. This one boat ramp is paved, and there is plenty of parking available. This is a free public ramp. This is a popular public launch into the main channel of the Trinity River. Expect power boat traffic and bank fisherman.

The Trinity River up-stream of Lake Livings-

ton has steep, muddy banks lined with trees.

A variety of game fish can be caught in this river including freshwater drum, striped bass, white bass, yellow bass, flathead catfish, channel catfish, blue catfish, as well as sunfish. The river meanders through isolated areas and is fed by numerous scenic creeks that provide abundant fish habitat. The river is wide and contains many sandbars that can be used for camping and day use.

There are no amenities at this launch.

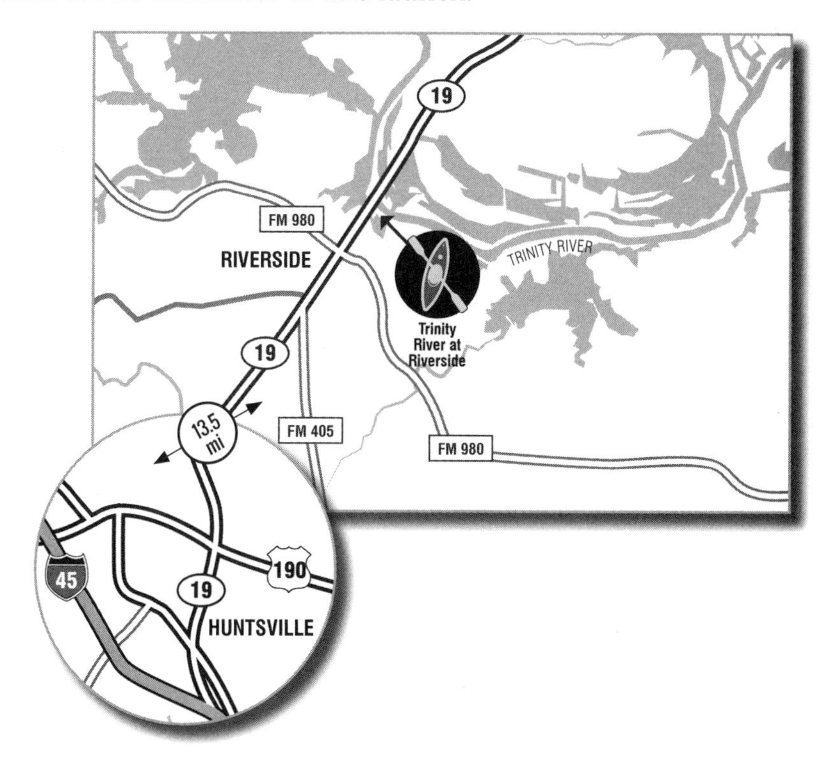

Harmon Creek Marina

14 Marina Point Drive

N 30 51.414, W 95 26.500 **Elevation: 144 feet**

TAKE I-45 NORTH to Huntsville, Texas, exit 113 to Hwy 19. Turn right on Hwy 19, continue 10.7 miles to Conoco gas station on the right. Take the next crossover and U turn. Turn right on the first street, Wood Farm Road. Follow the yellow signs to the marina, five miles. It is very well marked. Two paved launches here, and they charge $3 for kayaks. The area was very clean and mowed. The marina is in a protected cove and easy to use.

There is plenty of parking.

Paddle left out of the marina. Everything to the right dead ends. The short paddle out to Harmon Creek is easy and has a no-wake zone posted. We even had a couple of power boats launch after us, and they did idle (no wake) out to the main creek. The main creek is wide enough for boat traffic. We were there on the Sunday before Memorial Day and only saw

two boats in two hours. The creek does offer a good bit of protection. Harmon Creek is famous for catfish and white bass, gar and panfish. I fished a little white grub and landed a small bass and a white bass. This is great water for kayak fishing.

The water is also very agreeable for just kayaking. This creek eventually feeds into the Trinity River.

This marina is billed as the "best kept secret in the world," and it may be. It has all the amenities, including cabins, RV park, store and a playground. The folks were very friendly and helpful. It would be a nice weekend getaway.

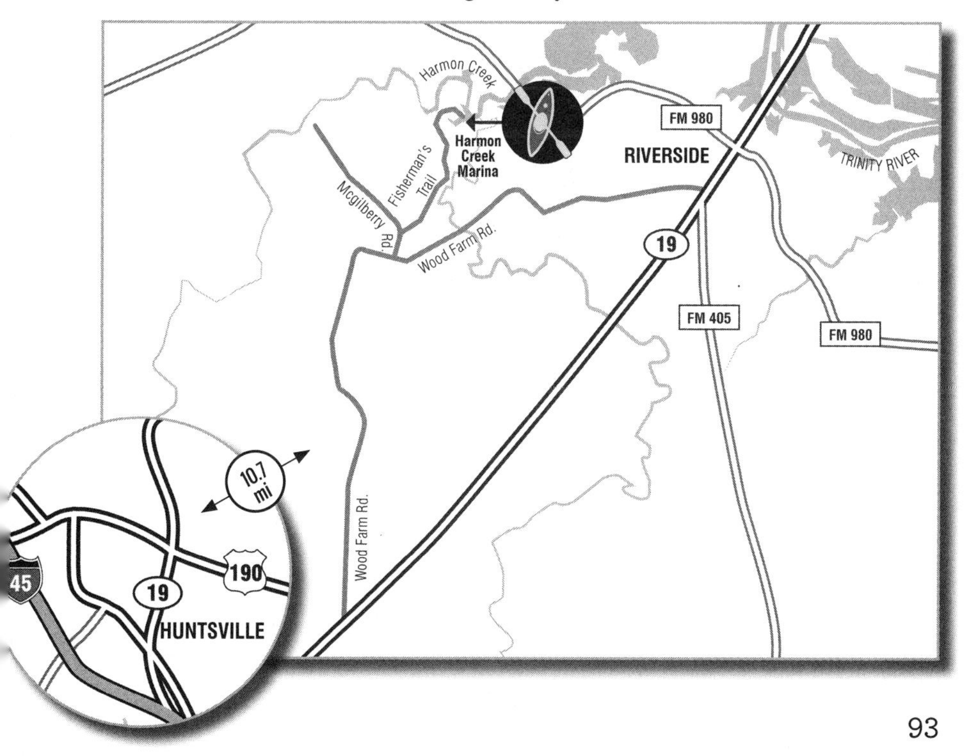

LAKE PINKSTON

THIS LAKE HAS 447 surface acres with an average depth of 20 feet. The lake was impounded in 1976.

Two sites are profiled on Lake Pinkston.

Lake Pinkston Dam 96

Lake Pinkston East 98

Lake Pinkston Dam

N 31 42.607, W 94 21.778 Elevation: 301 feet

From the intersection of Hwy 59 north and Sam Houston Parkway north (Beltway 8), travel Highway 59 north, 125 miles to loop 224 in Nacogdoches. Turn right (east) on Loop 224 and continue 4.2 miles to Highway 7. Turn right on 7, travel 18.1 miles to County Road 1234 and turn left on this dirt road. There are no signs showing access to this lake.

In just .3 miles, bear right at the Y onto County Road 1510 and continue two miles back to the dam. The road goes across the dam, and the launch is on the far side on the right.

This is a free, paved launch. It is only one lane, and parking is available on both sides of the road.

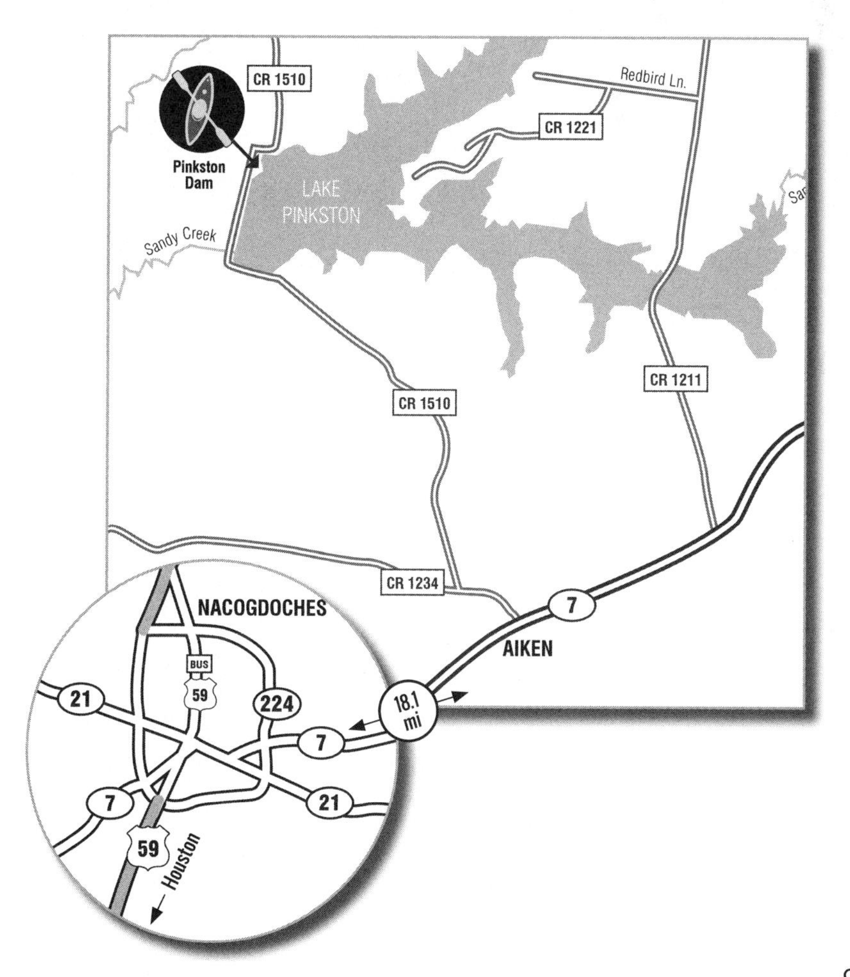

Lake Pinkston East

N 31 42.279, W 94 20.205 Elevation: 302 feet

FROM THE INTERSECTION of Hwy 59 north and Sam Houston Parkway north (Beltway 8), travel Highway 59 north, 125 miles to loop 224 in Nacogdoches. Turn right (east) on loop 224 4.2 miles to Highway 7. Turn right, travel 18.8 miles to County Road 1210 and turn left (CR 1211) onto this dirt road. There are no signs showing access to this lake. Continue one mile back to the lake.

There is a launch point on both sides of the road.

This has to be one of my favorite spots to paddle. One reason is, there are no jet skis allowed. The lake is a divided into two fingers with lots of flooded timber and submerged brush. Because of the long, protected shoreline, you can always get out of the wind. Lake Pinkston is primarily a largemouth bass and crappie lake. The lake record bass is 16.9 pounds. Share a Lunker bass were stocked in 2006 and 2008. The water here is generally clear to stained. It is fed by Sandy Creek, and the lake levels can fluctuate from one to five feet. There are no restrooms or other facilities at this site. There are very limited stores once you leave Nacogdoches. Bring what you need when you head out here.

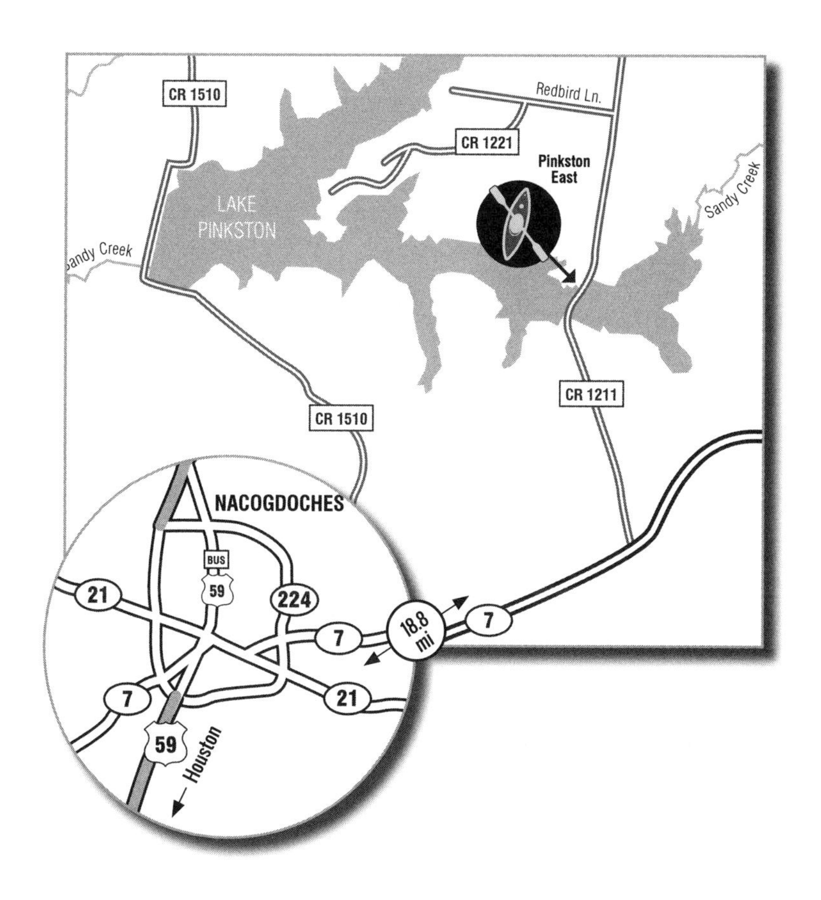

LAKE NACOGDOCHES

LAKE NACOGDOCHES IS located eight miles west of the Piney Woods city it is named for. It has 2,212 surface acres with a maximum depth of 40 feet. It was impounded in 1976.

Two launch sites are profiled on the lake.

Eastside Park 102

Westside Park 102

Lake Nacogdoches, Eastside Park

127925 S. FM 225

N 31 35.306, W 94 49.298 102 Elevation: East 305 feet

Lake Nacogdoches, Westside Park

127905 S. FM 225

N 31 35.590, W 94 50.251 102 Elevation: West 302 feet

From the intersection of Hwy 59 and Sam Houston Parkway north (Beltway 8), continue north on Hwy 59, 125 miles to loop 224 in Nacogdoches. Turn left (west) on Loop 224 and continue 1.5 miles. Exit to FM 225 and turn left 8.3 miles to the Eastside Park entrance on the right.

To launch on the west side of the lake, travel 9.5 miles on FM 225, to the Westside Park Launch on the right.

On the east side, there is plenty of paved parking available. This is a long, steep ramp with only one lane, but it has a nice turnaround at the bottom of the ramp so you don't have to back all the way down. The east-side ramp has a dock available.

The west side also has a long, steep ramp with only one lane. The park on the west side has a fishing pier that is handicap accessible. The two launch points are on either side of the dam.

These are the only public access, so you will paddle north away from the dam. There are several homes along the lake shore and plenty of docks to fish around. Not much flooded timber at the south end of the lake, but you'll find 16 miles of shoreline to explore. Largemouth bass crappie, catfish and bluegill are all plentiful. The lake record bass is 14.02/lbs. Over 450,00 Florida bass have been stocked in the last four years. There are many coves and protected areas to fish. Restrooms are available at this site. There is also a swimming and picnic area on the east side park that is handicap accessible. There is no store in the park, but there is one just at the entrance to the park on FM 225.

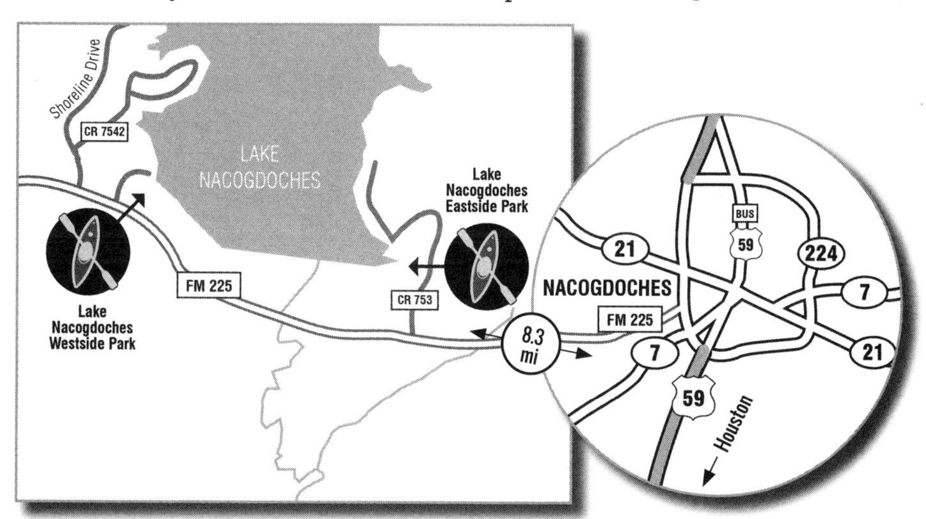

NECHES RIVER NORTH

THERE ARE TWO locations profiled from the Neches River North area.

Anderson Crossing	106
Highway 7	108

Anderson Crossing CR 1155
Davy Crockett Paddling Trail
N 31 26.676, W 95 02.052 106 Elevation: 190 feet

FROM LOOP 287 west in Lufkin, Texas , travel 12.3 miles west on SH 103/SH 7 to the Neches River. Continue 4.6 miles west on SH 7 to FS Road 511. Turn right on FS 511 and travel 2.3 miles to the stop sign at CR 1155. Turn right on CR 1155 and travel 2.7 miles to the river. These roads are gravel and very narrow. Proceed slowly with caution. There are two small bridges before you get to Anderson Crossing. Anderson Crossing has a small boat launch on the right side of the bridge. It is not a paved launch. The narrow path is sandy and rough. Parking here is very limited.

The Neches River in this area is not very wide and is relatively easy to paddle. The paddle trail suggests you put in here and

float about nine miles down to the take-out at the Hwy 7 launch. There may be snags or logjams that require portage. This stretch of water is home to the annual Neches River Rendezvous. A family-friendly event hosted by the Lufkin/Angeline County Chamber of Commerce and Temple Inland. The event is usually held the first week of June.

All native river fish would apply here. Bluegill, crappie, bass and plenty of catfish will be available here. Buffalo (fish) and gar are also very prevalent.

As with all rivers, check the flow before you head out. The water is a reddish, muddy color. Depending on the river flow this trip to Hwy 7 could take from 3-6 hours.

No amenities here. There are no restrooms. This location is somewhat remote. Take what you need.

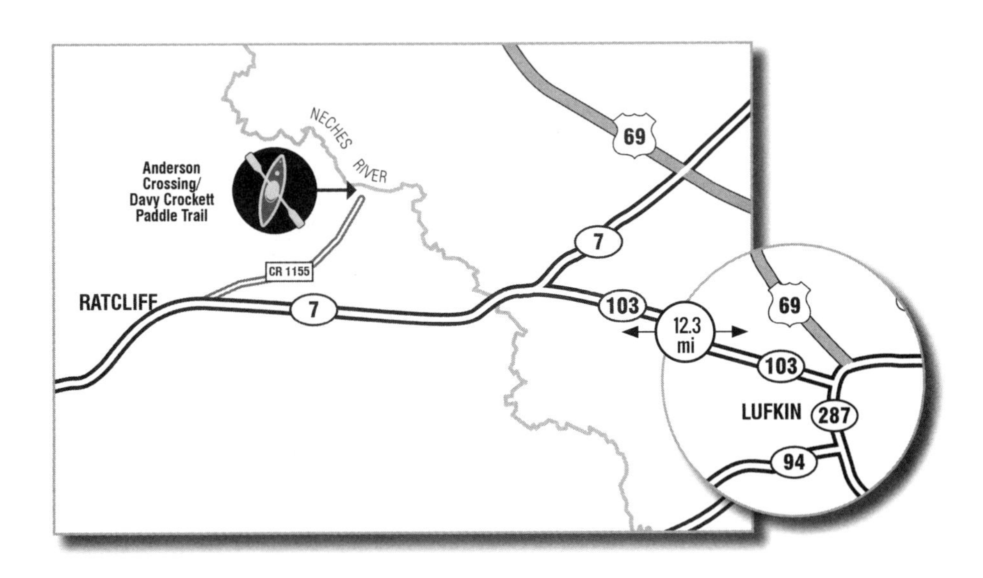

Highway 7

7097 Hwy 7, Pollok, Texas

N 31 23.797, W 94 57.929 Elevation: 179 feet

TRAVEL 12.3 MILES west of loop 287 in Lufkin, Texas on State Hwy 103. The river access is on the left. The small side road is Frank Ashby Rd.

This launch is somewhat paved. It has an asphalt base. There is plenty of parking available under the bridge.

The Neches River in this area is not very wide and is relatively easy to

paddle. The paddle trail suggests you put in about nine miles north and float down to this take-out. This spot would be fine to go for an upstream paddle and float back as well.

No amenities here. No restrooms and no stores available once you leave Lufkin.

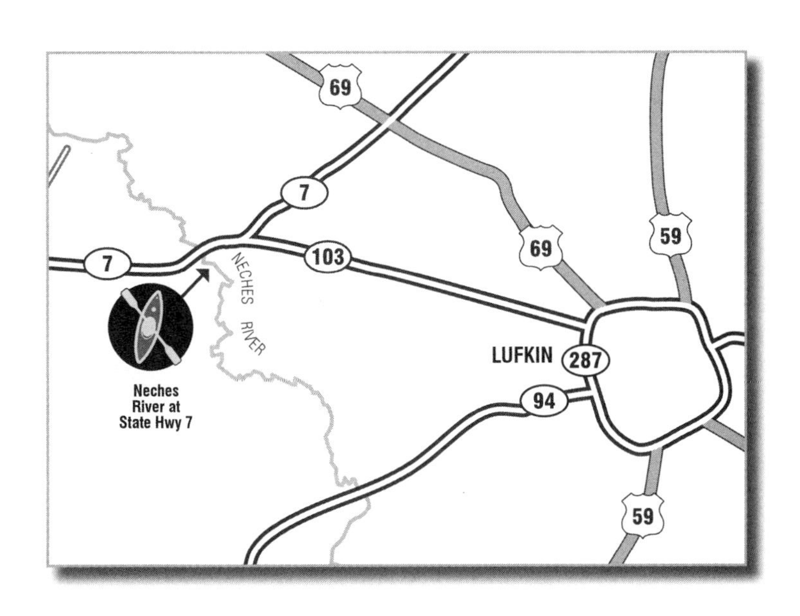

BA STEINHAGEN LAKE

WE MAPPED 12 different launches on this lake. They are maintained by both the TPWD and the Corps of Engineers. Directions are given from the intersection of Hwy 92 and 190 which is 12.4 miles east of Woodville. This intersection is between Woodville and Jasper on the west side of the lake.

All the ramps listed here are paved. Many of them have nearby restrooms, shelters, camping, piers and fish cleaning stations.

Magnolia 1	112
Magnolia 2	113
Campers Cove Park	114
Cherokee 1	116
Cherokee 2	118
Tidelands Ramp	120
Walnut Ridge	122
Hen House Ridge	124
Hen House Canoe Launch	125
Sandy Creek 1	127
Sandy Creek 2	128
Sandy Creek 3	129
Sandy Creek 4	130

LAUNCH POINTS ON THE WEST SIDE OF THE LAKE:

Magnolia Ridge Park
N 30 52.232, W 94 14.062 Elevation: 90 feet

FROM THE INTERSECTION of Hwy 190 and FM 92, take FM 92 north one mile. Turn right on CR 3700. There is a brown state sign here. Continue one mile on CR 3700, to the park entrance. This is a Corps of Engineers park and has a daily entry fee of $3.

Magnolia 1

THE FIRST RAMP is on the right before you enter the park gate. I was told it is free to launch here. The water at this ramp was pretty shallow but looked like enough to launch a kayak. It was a short paddle out through the cypress trees to the lake. There is plenty of paved parking.

Magnolia 2

THIS RAMP IS located inside the park. $3 entrance fee, launch included. The water is much deeper here. Still there are a few cypress trees along the shore. The park has restrooms, camping and hiking trails. I saw lots of wildlife and birds visible in the park. This ramp also has plenty of paved parking.

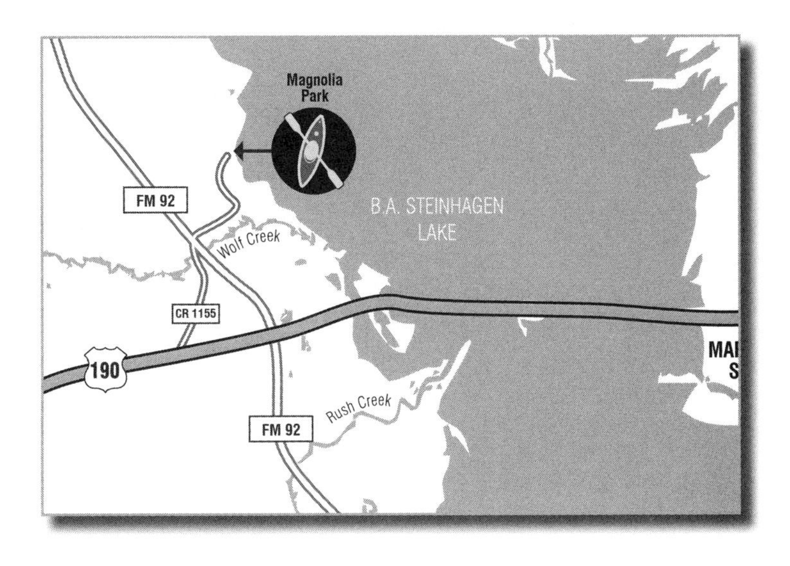

Campers Cove Park

525 Campers Cove Road, Woodville, Texas

N 30 49.534, W 94 12.345 Elevation: 123 feet

FROM THE INTERSECTION of Hwy 190 and FM 92, take FM 92 south 2.5 miles to CR 4130 and turn left. There is no sign for the ramp only the small county road sign. Travel .5 miles to a Y and

stay right. The road will dead end at the ramp on your left in .5 miles. This is a paved ramp with plenty of shoreline to explore. No amenities at this ramp. A $3 daily fee is required.

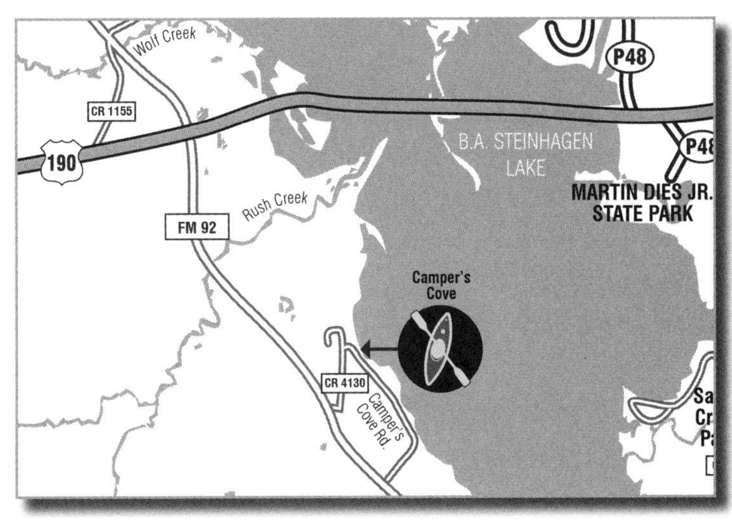

Cherokee 1

N 30 51.257, W 94 12.859 Elevation: 63 feet

From the intersection of Hwy 190 and FM 92, continue east on Hwy 190, .8 miles. This launch is on the very west end of the bridge. Turn left into the parking lot. A big, brown, wood state sign identifies this ramp.

The ramp is paved, and the day I was here there were several trailers in the parking area. This spot looks to be a popular power boat launch. A short paddle out to the right will put

you on the main lake, north of the bridge. A $3 daily fee is required. No amenities at this ramp.

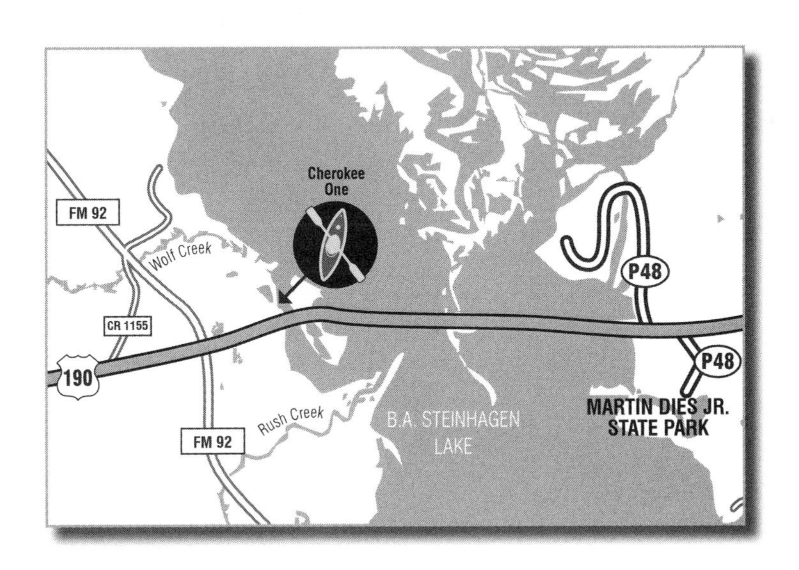

Cherokee 2

N 30 51.103, W 94 12.613 Elevation: 57 feet

From the intersection of Hwy 190 and FM 92, continue east .8 mile. This launch is on the very west end of the bridge. A big, brown, wood state sign identifies this entrance. Turn right and travel .2 mile to the ramp.

This ramp is on the south side of the bridge and has a very large paved lot. This ramp is

also paved. A short paddle straight across will put you along a cypress island in the middle of the lake. No amenities at this ramp.

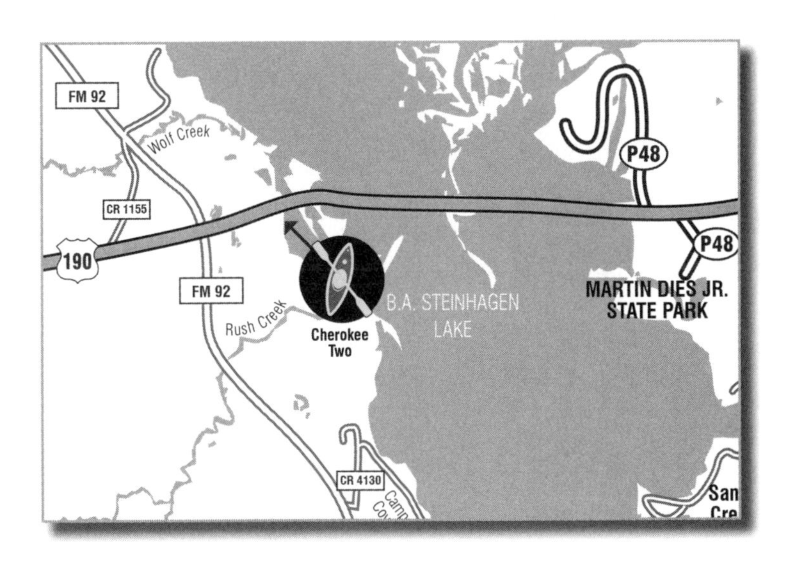

LAUNCHES ON THE EAST SIDE OF THE LAKE:

Tidelands Ramp

N 30 51.158, W 94 10.362 Elevation: 78 feet

From the intersection of Hwy 190 and FM 92, travel east on Hwy 190, continue across the bridge 3.4 miles. At the east end of the bridge immediately on the right is the entrance to the Tidelands ramp. To the left is the entrance to Walnut Creek on Park Road 48 north.

Tidelands ramp is paved and has a smaller

parking area. It also has a small fishing pier. If you want to fish the bridge area this looks to be a great place to launch.

Within a short paddle you can cross under the bridge and go north or fish the bridge pilings.

There are no amenities at this ramp.

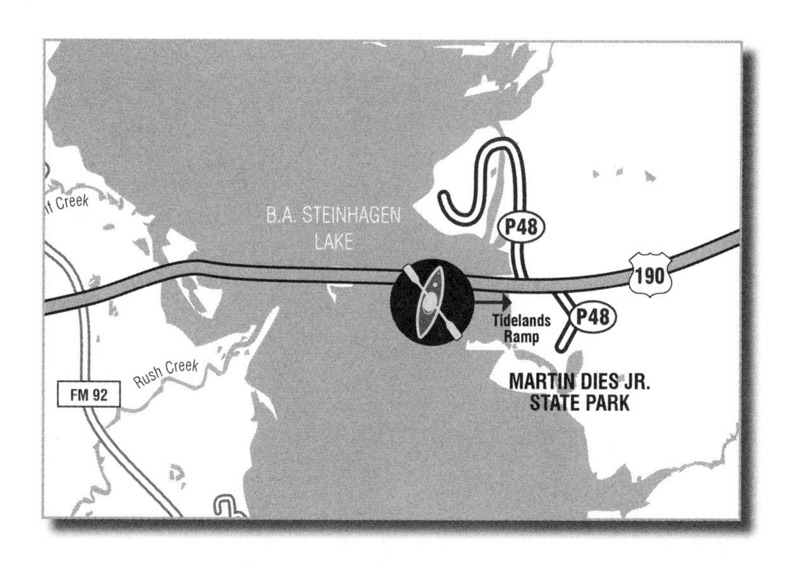

Walnut Ridge

N 30 51.774, W 94 10.945 Elevation: 66 feet

From the intersection of 190 and FM 92 travel east on Hwy 190, continue across the bridge 3.4 miles. At the end of the bridge, turn to the left on Park Road 48 north. Travel 1.8 miles north to the ramp. Stay on the main road and it will go directly to the ramp. A $3 entrance fee is required.

This launch area is part of the Texas Paddling Trail. The trail map is provided at the

launch. There are also canoes for rent here on site. This launch is inside the park, so are the restrooms, and a nice fish cleaning station. There are several shelters for rent here and a fishing pier that is separate from the ramp area. This seemed to be a more protected area of the lake.

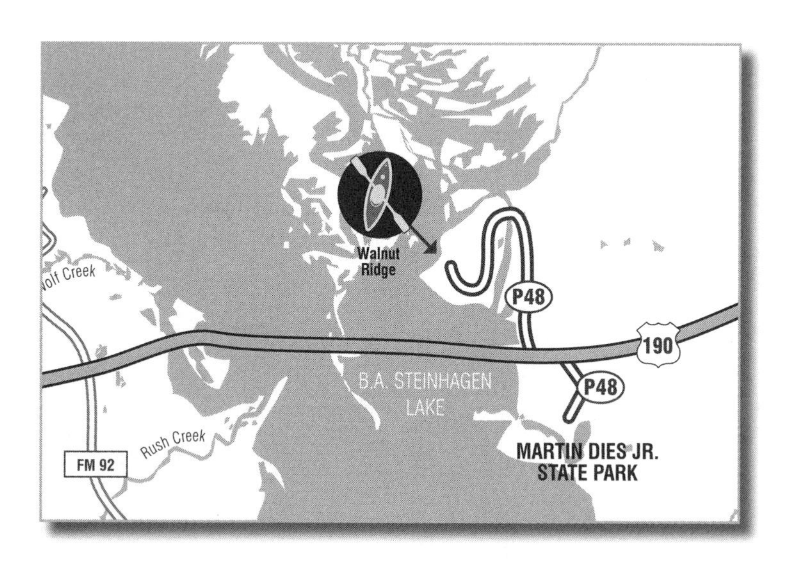

Hen House Ridge

N 30 50.574, W 94 10.465 Elevation: 65 feet

FROM THE INTERSECTION of Hwy 190 and FM 92, continue east on Hwy 190, across the bridge 3.9 miles. You will pass the entrance sign for Walnut Ridge and Tidelands. Turn right on Park Road 48 south. This is the main office for Martin Dies State Park. They have a park store and friendly folks (during working hours) who can help you decide where to go. Camping and shelters are available along with canoe rental. Restrooms, hot showers, hiking,

biking, and interpretative nature trails are available here as well. A $3 entry fee is required. Follow the main road to the ramp .5 miles in the campground. This is a paved ramp and it is well into the main body of the lake. There is a lot of open water to paddle here. A fish cleaning station is very near the ramp along with restrooms close by. There is plenty of paved parking here.

Hen House Canoe Launch

THIS ACCESS IS inside Martin Dyes State park. Travel **.3 MILES FROM** the park entrance, and there is a kayak / canoe launch with a floating dock. The launch is in a more secluded cypress tree-filled area and allows you to make a short paddle in a protected part of the lake.

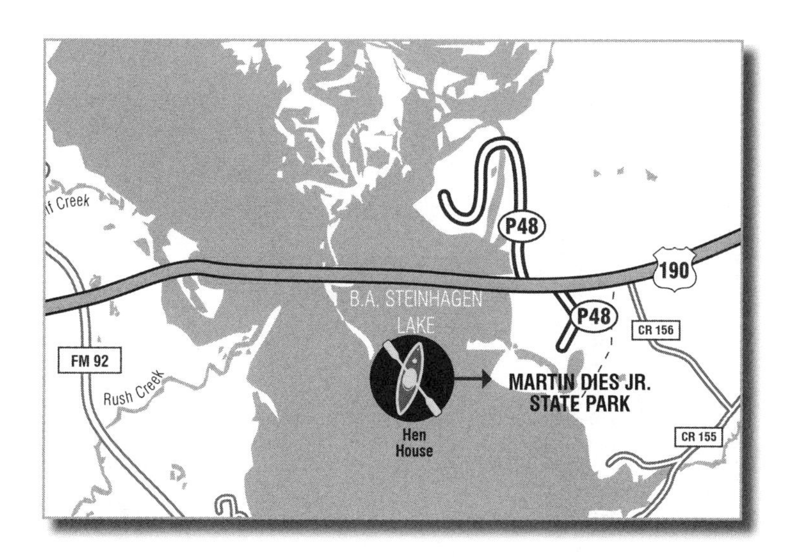

Sandy Creek Park

From the intersection of Hwy 190 and FM 92, continue east 4.4 miles on Hwy 190. Turn right on county road 156. There is no park sign here, only a small county road sign. It is the first right after you pass Park Road 48 south, the entrance to Martin Dies SP. Go south on CR 156, 1.4 miles to a T in the road, turn right (west). Continue .6 miles to a low water crossing, and continue .5 miles to the park gate on the right.

This is a US Army Corps of Engineers park and includes four different launching points. This park has lots of really nice shelters and restrooms. The ramps are all paved and well maintained. There is a $3 entrance fee required. This park is a little farther south on the lake than all the others, but looked to be great spots to launch from.

Sandy Creek 1 Kayak/Canoe
N 30 49.778, W 94 09.180 Elevation: 108 feet

As you enter the park, this launch is .4 miles on your right. This access is back in a protected channel off the main lake. It is a great spot to launch without having to share the ramp with any power boats. It has a nice floating dock, but you will have to navigate 25-30 yards of open ground to get to the water. There are no obstructions, so it should be no problem. It is well-marked with a sign that denotes canoe/kayak launch.

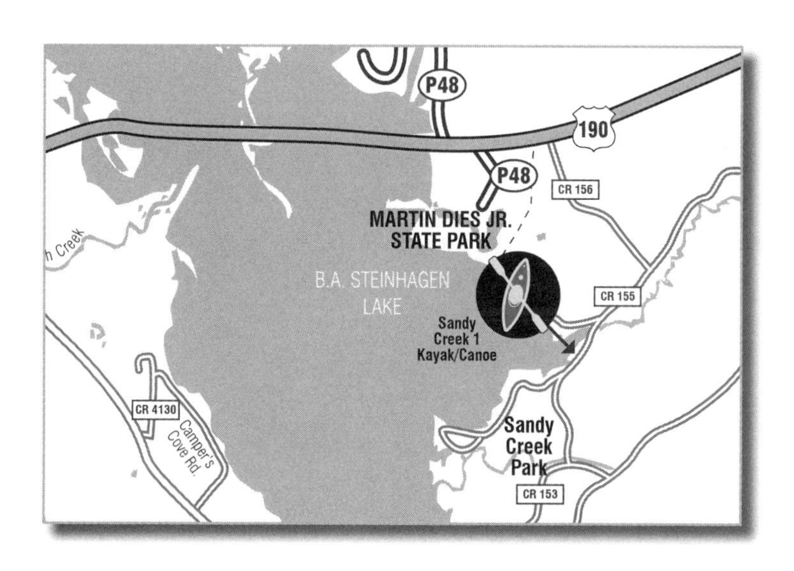

Sandy Creek 2

N 30 49.645, W 94 09.669   Elevation: 77 feet

THIS RAMP IS inside the park and is on the main park road. **THE LAUNCH IS** on the main body of the lake with lots of open water to paddle. It is paved and has a fishing pier just to the left.

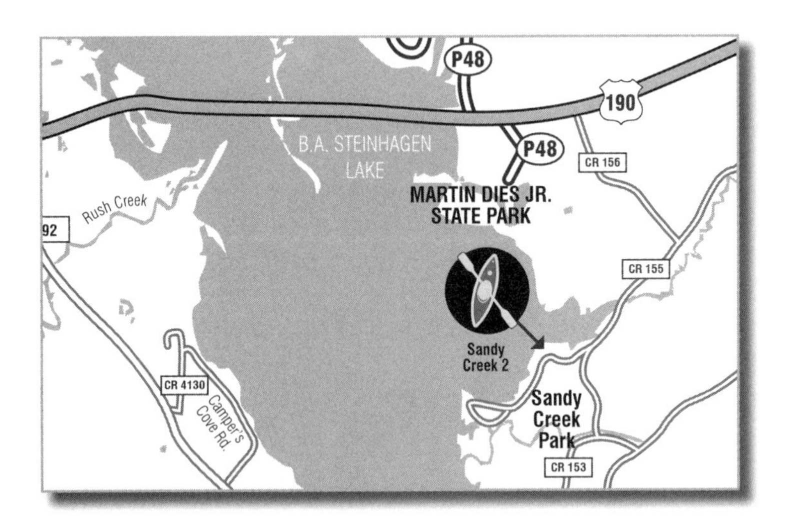

Sandy Creek 3

N 30 49.645, W 94 09.669 Elevation: 55 feet

THIS RAMP IS farther south on the main park road, located on a peninsula. It is a more protected launch area but a short paddle will get you out into the main lake. This is the farthest south public launch we found. This is a paved ramp and has plenty of paved parking. Restrooms are close by.

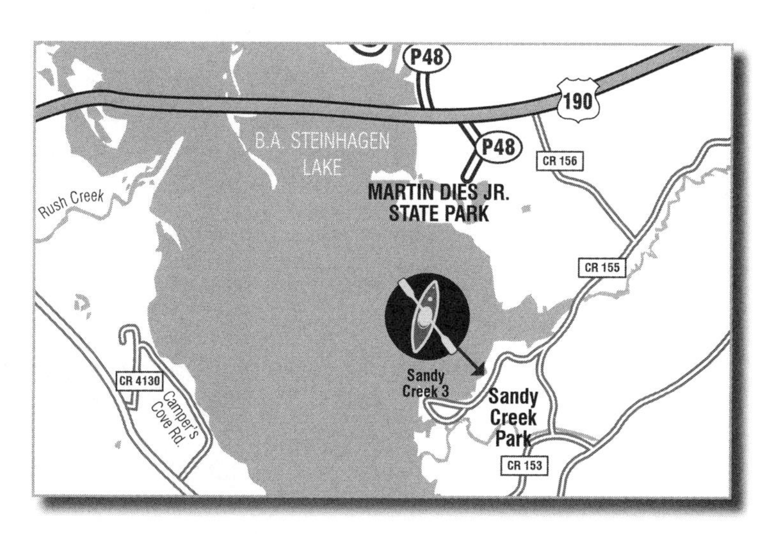

Sandy Creek 4

N 30 49.893, W 94 09.553 Elevation: 77 feet

THIS RAMP IS before you get to the main gate of the park. When you get to the low water crossing you will see a sign for campsites that are north along the lake. Turn right here and travel .5 miles to the ramp. It is across the bay from Sandy Creek 2 ramp. This ramp is also paved but does have somewhat limited paved parking.

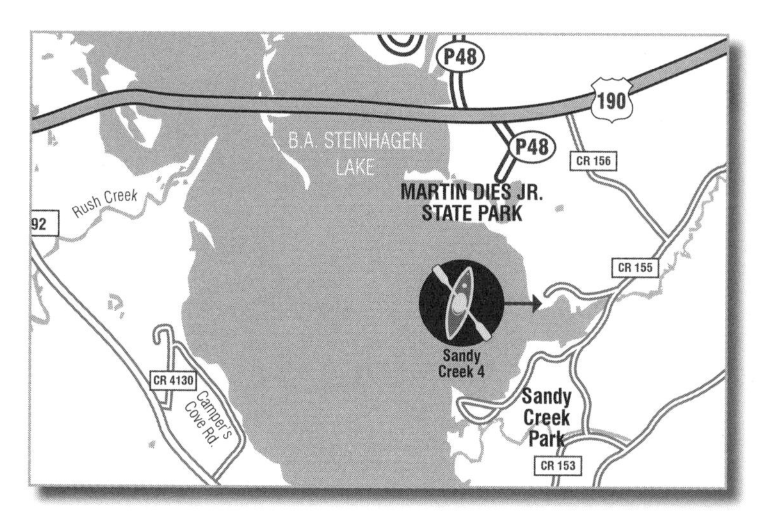
P48
190
B.A. STEINHAGEN
LAKE
P48
CR 156
MARTIN DIES JR.
STATE PARK
Rush Creek
92
CR 155
Sandy
Creek 4
CR 4130
Camper's
Cove Rd.
Sandy
Creek
Park
CR 153

BIG THICKET VILLAGE CREEK LOWER NECHES

ELEVEN LAUNCH SITES are profiled from this area in southeast Texas between the Trinity River near Cleveland and the Neches River at Beaumont.

FM 418 Launch on Village Creek	134
FM 327 Launch on Village Creek	136
Baby Galvez Launch on Village Cr.	138
Hwy 96 Crossing on Village Creek	140
Village Creek State Park	142
Pine Island Bayou Launch	146
LNVA Saltwater Barrier	147
Collier's Ferry Park	148
Evadale Launch Neches River	150
County Park Launch Neches River	152
Cleveland/105 Launch	154

FM 418 Launch on Village Creek

N 30 23.870, W 94 15.899 Elevation: 43 feet

From the intersection of FM 326 and Hwy 69/287 in Kountze, Texas, continue north on 69/287, .7 miles and turn right on FM 418. Travel east 3.3 miles to Village Creek. The launch is on the right before you cross the bridge.

The ramp is paved almost all the way to the water, and you have a nice sand bank to launch from.

The creek in this area is about 50 yards

wide, with plenty of sand bars. This creek is a very winding float. There is limited parking here. On the north side of 418 is a county park with a sandy area to picnic.

No amenities here, but they do have trash cans.

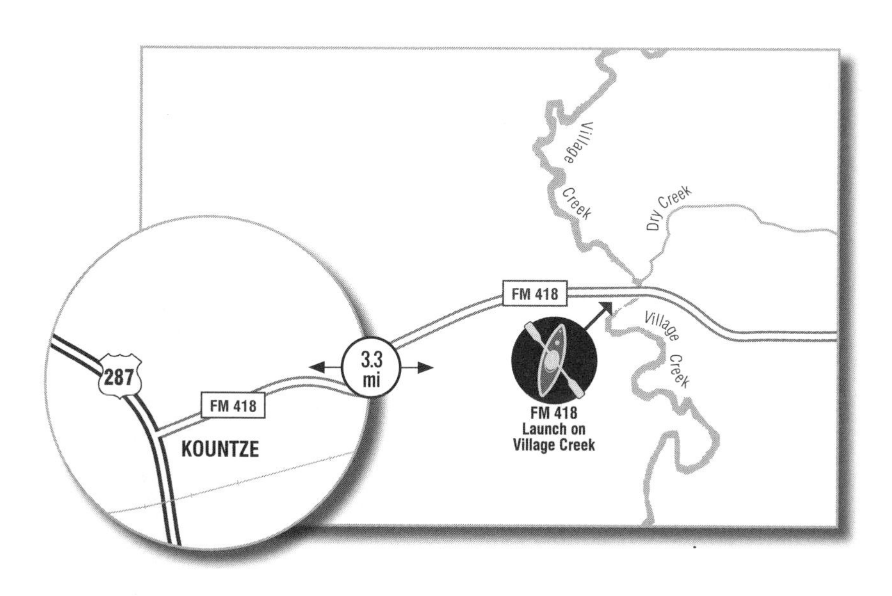

SH 327 Launch on Village Creek

N 30 20.821 W 94 14.361 Elevation: 53 feet

From the intersection of FM 326 and Hwy 69/287 in Kountze, Texas, travel south on 69/287, 1.5 miles and turn left on State Highway 327. Travel east 2.2 miles, and the launch is on the right before you cross the bridge.

It is a steep exit road off the highway. The road is paved and makes a loop under the bridge back to the north side of FM 327.

The launch is a nice sand bank.

There is limited parking here. Village Creek is a bit wider here. Looks like a great paddle. There are no amenities here, only trash cans.

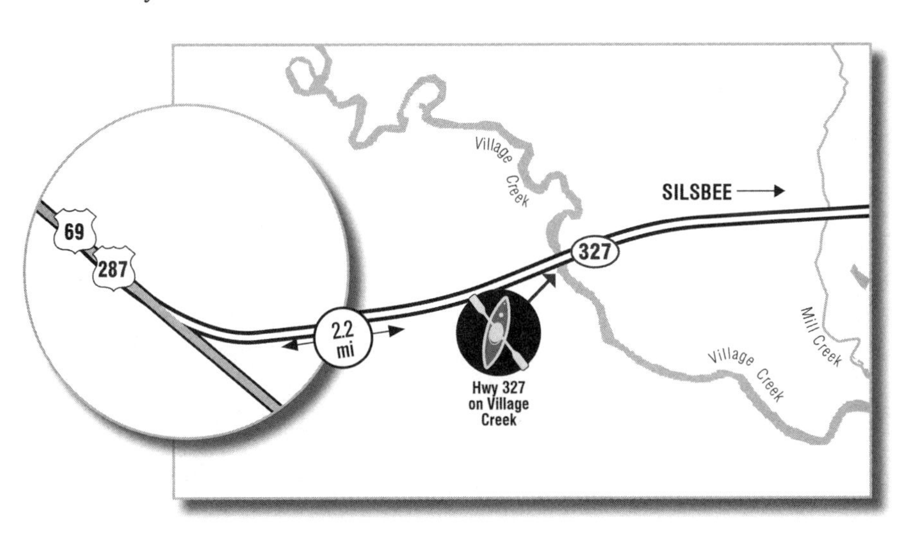

Baby Galvez Launch on Village Creek
N 30 20.064 W 94 12.232 Elevation: 26 feet

FROM THE INTERSECTION of State Highway 327 and US 96 Business in downtown Silsbee, Texas travel south on 96 Bus, .8 miles to Maxwell Ave and turn right. Travel .1 miles to Lindsey, turn left. Travel .9 miles on Lindsey, and it will dead end into Baby Galvez Rd. (no sign). Turn left on Baby Galvez Rd. for .2 miles to the launch.

There is another way

in to this launch off Kiwanis Club Rd., but if you have never been here before, stick with the directions off Lindsey. This is a one-lane paved ramp with plenty of parking. The parking area is mostly sand. No amenities, but there are trash cans here.

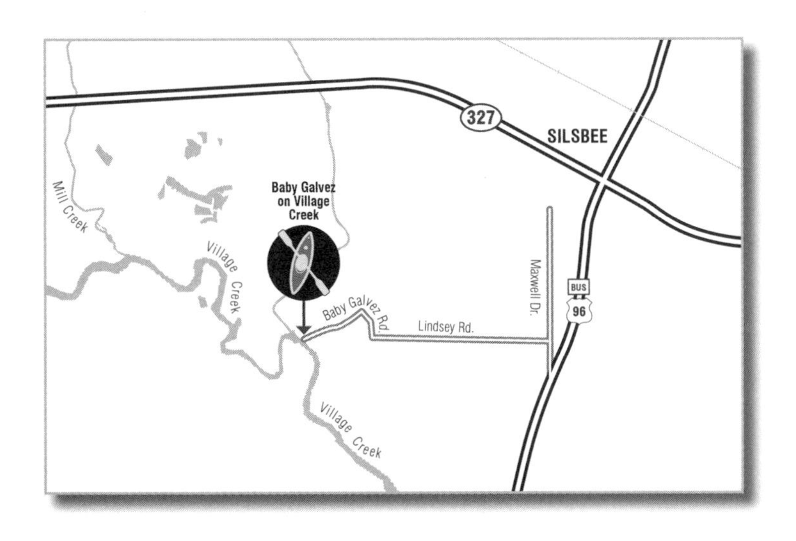

Hwy 96 Crossing Launch on Village Creek

N 30 17.144, W 94 11.486 Elevation: -3 feet

From the intersection of FM 327 and US 96 Business in downtown Silsbee, Texas, travel south on US 96 Bus., 3.9 miles to the exit for the launch. It is marked with a public boat ramp sign. Make a U-turn under the bridge and follow the paved road to the launch. This site has lots of

room and plenty of parking. There is a one-lane paved ramp here.

There are no amenities here, only trash cans.

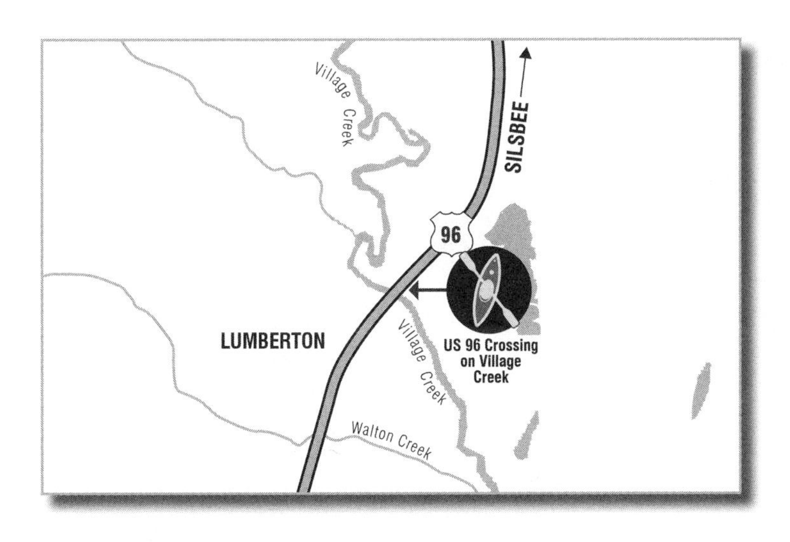

Village Creek State Park

8854 Park Road 74, Lumberton, TX 77657

N 30 15.292 W 94 10.276 Elevation: 28 feet

From the intersection of FM 327 and US 96 Business in downtown Silsbee, Texas, travel south on 96, 5.6 miles to Lumberton, Texas. Turn left, east on E Chance Rd. .5 miles to FM 3513 (Village Creek Parkway) and turn right. Travel south on FM 3513 1.2 miles and turn left at Tram Road. Cross the railroad tracks and immediately veer

left onto Alma Drive. Travel east on Alma approximately 1/4 mile to the park entrance.

As with most state parks it is well-marked, and the signs are very visible. There is a daily entrance fee of $3 per day

Follow the main park road to the parking area. The launch is at the very left end of the parking lot. The trees kind of hide the creek. There is not a formal boat ramp here, but a short portage of about 50 yards gets you to a nice sand bank to launch from. Under normal conditions, Village Creek is much wider and slower here.

You should be able to paddle upstream from this launch point. There are showers and restrooms in the building just inside the park gate, but this is the only one. The parking lot restrooms are porta-cans. This park is well-maintained and should be on everyone's short list of places to paddle.

There are four local kayak/canoe outfitters who can help with equipment rental and shuttle service. These outfitters are also a wealth of knowledge about the rivers. I highly recommend you check with one of these folks, they will help make your trip more enjoyable.

Big Thicket Outfitters
409-786-1884 **www.bigthicketoutfitters.com**

Eastex Canoe Rentals
409-385-4700 **www.eastexcanoes.com**

Pineywoods Outfitters
409-751-0911 **www.canoetexas.com**

Sharps Canoe and Kayak
409-385-6241 **www.sharpcanoerental.com**

Estimated travel times are listed as:

418 to 327	8.6 miles	4-6 hours*
327 to Baby Galvez	2.1 miles	1-2 hours*
Baby Galvez to US 96	7.1 miles	3-5 hours*
US 96 to Village Creek SP	3.2 miles	1-3 hours*

*Paddle times are only estimates and can vary due to water levels, flow rates and portages. Heavy rains can cause very dangerous conditions. Always check stream flow information before planning a trip.

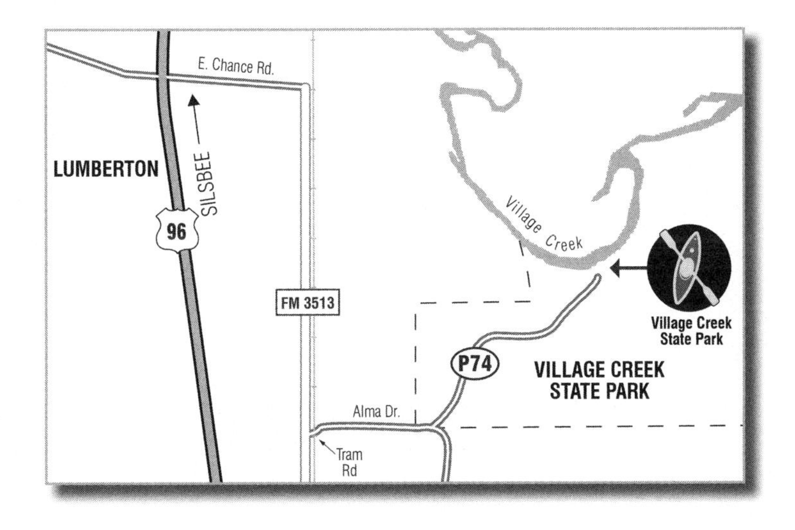

Pine Island Bayou Launch

N 30 10.771 W 94 11.195 Elevation: 23 feet

From the intersection of FM 3513 south and US 69/287/96, continue south on US 69, 2.7 miles to Cooks Lake Road exit. Stay on the feeder southbound, and the ramp is on the U-turn under the bridge.

This is a one-lane, paved ramp. The bayou is pretty muddy here but winds around and connects with the Neches River above the Salt Water Lock system. No amenities here, only trash cans.

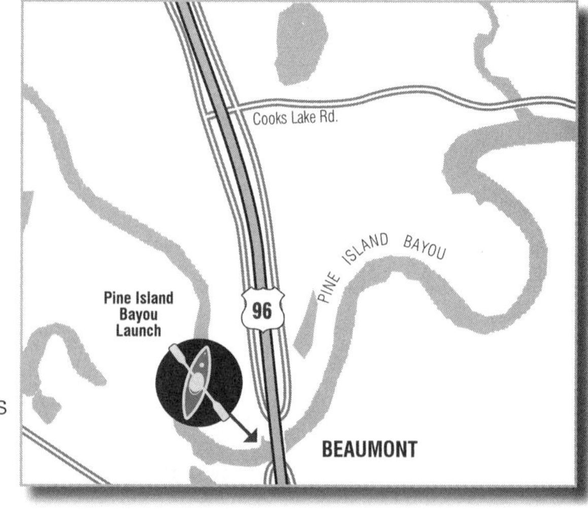

LNVA Salt Water Barrier Neches River

6700 Bigner Beaumont, Texas

N 30 09.320 W 94 06.961 Elevation: 1 foot

From the intersection of US 69 and E Lucas Dr., north of Beaumont, Texas, travel east .9 miles on E Lucas, to Bigner St. turn left and travel 1.5 miles to the gate of LNVA. Continue one mile to the two ramps.

The Lower Neches Valley Authority operates two boat ramps here. One is located on each side of the lock system. It is possible the locks may be closed, but with a ramp on either side you can launch at whichever side you wish to paddle. Both ramps are very well-maintained concrete, and restrooms are available at the north ramp. The parking lot for the south ramp is separate from the launch site.

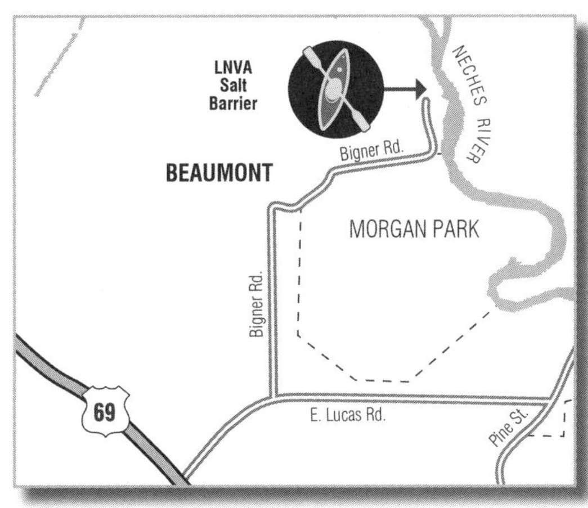

Collier's Ferry Park

5390 Pine St. Beaumont, Texas

N 30 07.929 W 94 05.751 Elevation: -5 feet

From the intersection of US 69 and E Lucas Dr., north of Beaumont, Texas, travel east on E Lucas, 2.9 miles to Pine Street and turn left. Travel .5 miles on Pine St. to the park entrance. The Neches River is very wide in this area, so wind will be a factor. This is the salt side of the

river, so brackish, coastal fishing conditions will apply. This park has four paved ramps, a pier, and is very well-maintained. There is also plenty of paved parking. This park has restrooms and a pavilion.

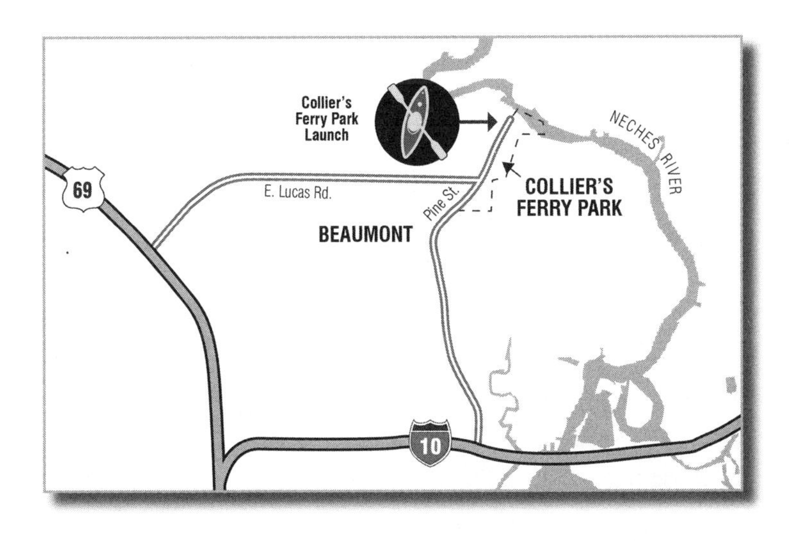

Evadale Launch   Neches River

N 30 21.378   W 94 05.679   Elevation: 9 feet

From the intersection of FM 327 and US 96, east of Silsbee, Texas, continue north on US 96, 3.7 miles toward Evadale, Texas. The launch will be on your right before you cross the river. This is a steep exit from the highway, so use caution if you are pulling a trailer.

There is a one-lane, paved ramp

with a nice sandy spot to launch from. Just south of the ramp is a picnic area with tables and parking. There is bank fishing access in the picnic area, but not really a place to launch from. No restrooms available here.

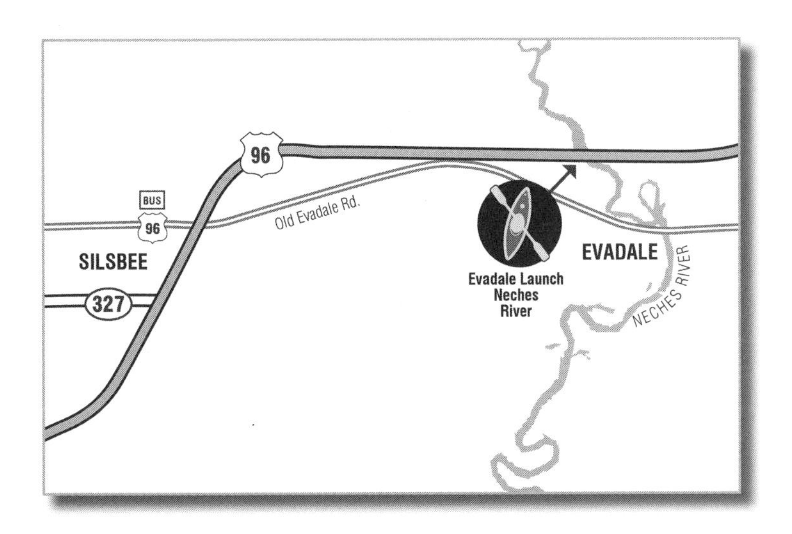

County Park Launch Neches River

N 30 25.686 W 94 06.954 Elevation: 35 feet

From the intersection of FM 418 and FM 92/96 Business in Silsbee, Texas, travel north on FM 92/96 Bus 3.8 miles to Cravens Camp Road and turn right. Travel 2.8 miles and stay right at the Y. Continue one mile, and you will dead end into the county park.

This launch is basically a big sand bar with a road to it. There are no signs and no amenities here. It is nice big sand bar with plenty of places to park and launch.

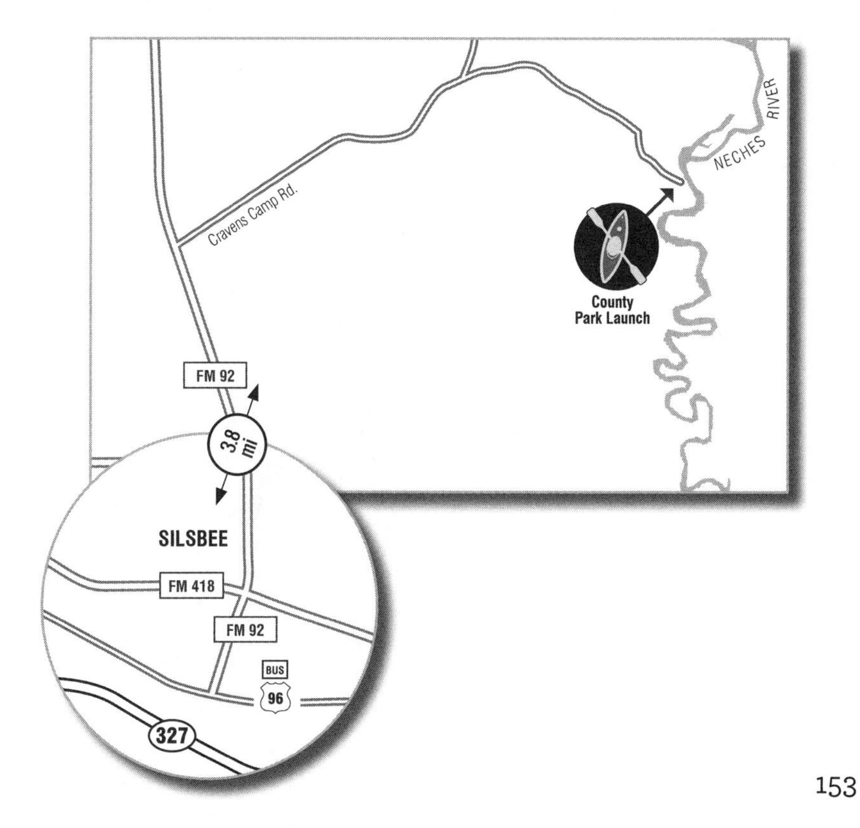

Cleveland/105 Launch
Trinity River
N 30 16.659, W 94 47.960 Elevation: 21 feet

From The intersection of US 59 and Hwy 105 in Cleveland, Texas travel east on 105, 18.6 miles to the Trinity River. There is no formal launch here, but parking and sand bars are located on the west side of the river. The "roads" leading to the river should be traveled at your own risk.

Several trucks had managed the drive down to the river's edge, the day I was there, but it was dry. If you stay parked on pavement up near the bridge, you are looking at a 200-yard portage to get to the water over mostly sand or very rough sandy roads. If you have a cart, bring it to this launch. No amenities located here.

COLORADO RIVER

THERE ARE FIVE locations profiled along the Colorado River and the San Bernard River in south central Texas.

SH 71 Business	159
Beasons Park	160
Hollywood Park	162
521 River Park	164
Hanson Riverside Park	166

Columbus, Texas Launch Sites

THESE TWO LAUNCHES in Columbus, are part of the Texas Paddling Trail. If you are planning this paddle, understand there are no intermediate take-out points along the river. This trail is 6.5 miles long with only one put-in and one take-out.

Paddle time estimates range from two to five hours depending on river flow rates and wind conditions. The land along the river is private property, and no-trespassing is enforced.

There is a local rental business and livery available.

HOWELL CANOE LIVERY
804 ROBSON ST. Columbus, TX 78934
PHONE: (979) 732-3816

State Hwy 71 Business
N 29 42.833, W 96 32.856 Elevation: 157 feet

From the intersection of I-10 and 71 Business, continue north on 71 Business 1.6 miles across the bridge and exit right. The exit for the launch is on the north side of the bridge. Turn right and travel back under the bridge. There is a public boat ramp sign at the exit. This is a one-lane, paved ramp, with some parking. This is a free launch.

No amenities available at this site.

Beasons Park

N 29 42.198, W 96 32.095 Elevation: 176 feet

FROM THE INTERSECTION of I-10 and 71 Business, continue north on 71 business one mile to Hwy 90. Turn right on 90 and travel .8 miles east to Beasons Park on the right. Stay to the right and travel to the launch/take-out site.

There is a gravel road down the bank

that will get you to within 30 yards of a nice sand bank to launch or take-out.

This is a Colorado County park, funded by both Texas Parks & Wildlife Department and Lower Colorado River Authority. It has restrooms, free parking and a pavilion.

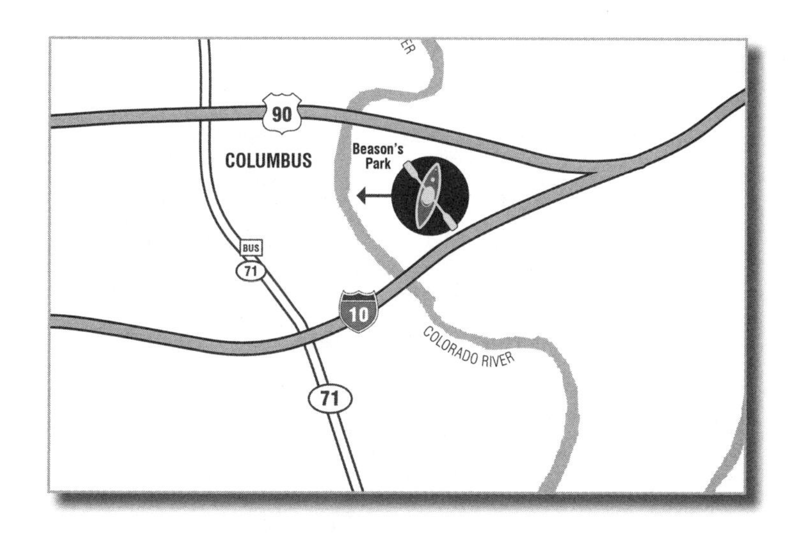

Hollywood Park

N 29 09.768, W 96 02.600 Elevation: 65 feet

From the intersection of Hwy 59 and FM 1162 in El Campo (one mile south of Pierce, Texas), continue south on FM 1162 to CR 444. Turn left on this gravel road and continue 5.7 miles. CR444 dead-ends into the park.

There are no amenities here and only one porta-can.

It is a free launch site The park is very nice and has a large sand beach along the river. You will need to portage down a small grass hill about 100 yards.

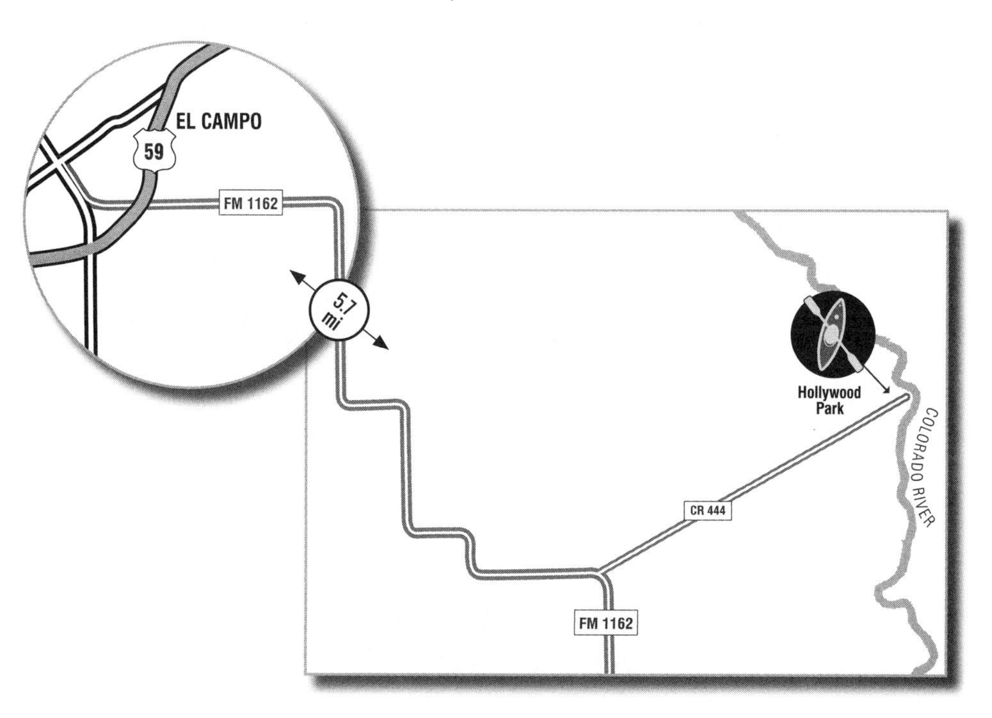

521 River Park Launch

N 28 47.252, W 95 59.780 **Elevation: 21 feet**

From the intersection of Hwy 35 and Hwy 60 in Bay City, Texas, continue south on Hwy 60, 12 miles and turn right on 521. Continue 2.3 miles across the Colorado river bridge and turn left to access the ramp.

A boat ramp sign marks the turn. There is no fee at this park.

A steep, paved ramp enters the river. There is no real bank space to launch from. Picnic tables, a pavilion and a pier, are available. Only one porta-can here for a restroom.

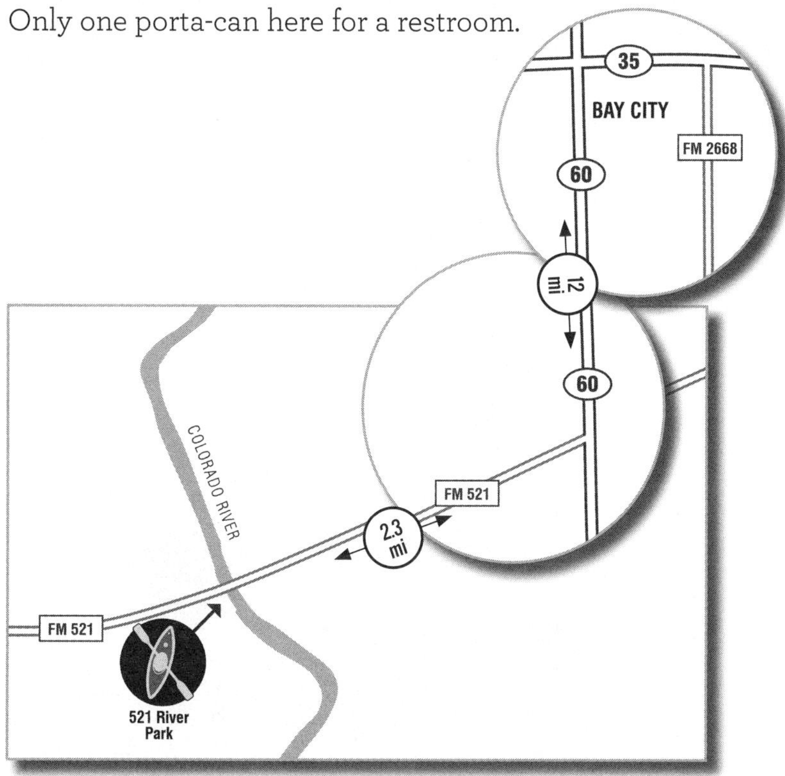

Hanson Riverside Park on the San Bernard River

N 29 06.761, W 95 40.489 Elevation: 12 feet

FROM THE INTERSECTION of Hwy 35 and Hwy 36 in West Columbia Texas, continue south on Hwy 35, three miles to the park entrance on your left, before you cross the river.

This is not a formal ramp. Access to the water is at the east end of the park. There are restrooms and

playground equipment available, along with plenty of picnic tables.

The San Bernard River is slow enough under normal conditions to be able to paddle both ways from the launch.

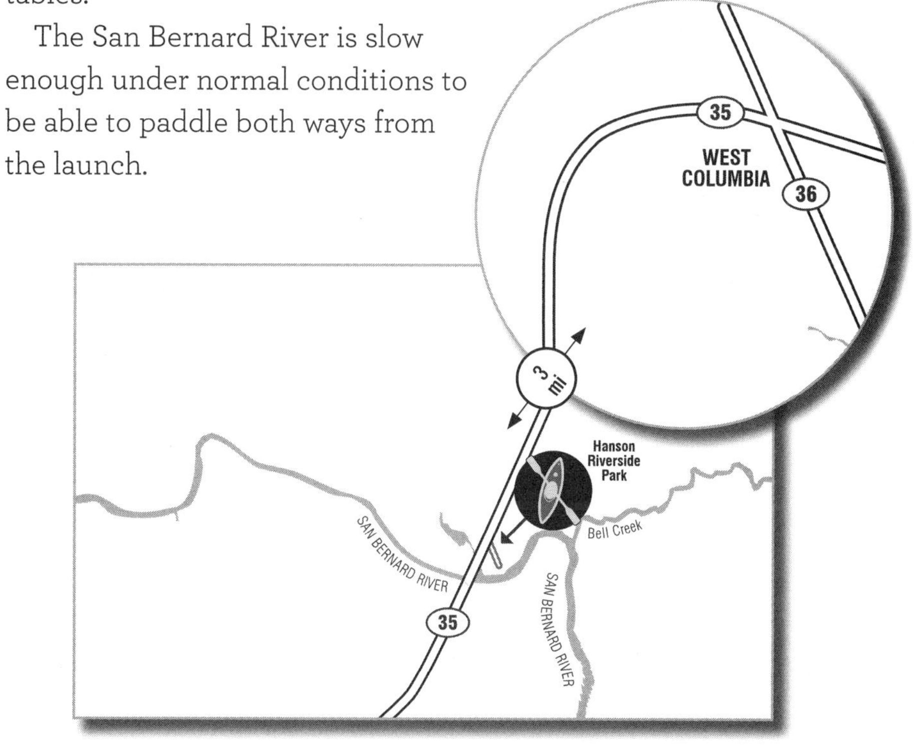

FAYETTE COUNTY RES.

FAYETTE COUNTY LAKE is a power plant cooling reservoir located 10 miles east of LaGrange Texas.

It is known as one of the top bass fishing locations in the state. Catfish and bluegills are also very plentiful in the lake. With a surface area of 2,400 acres it offers plenty of shoreline cover to fish and explore. Standing timber in the back coves makes for excellent kayak water. The best fishing is in late winter and early spring as the water is warmer than other bodies of water. Bass are most active between February and June.

Oak Thicket	170
Park Prairie	172

Oak Thicket

N 29 57.006, W 96 43.992   Elevation: 370 feet

At the intersection of Texas Highway 71 and FM 955, west of Ellinger, Texas, turn onto FM 955 and travel north 4.7 miles to the intersection of FM 955 and Texas Highway 159 in Fayetteville.

Turn left (west) on Hwy 159 and travel 4.3 miles to the park entrance.

There is a boat ramp sign showing the turn to Oak Thicket. Turn left and continue to the boat ramp. A $5 fee is required to use this park.

There are restrooms a pier and picnic tables available.

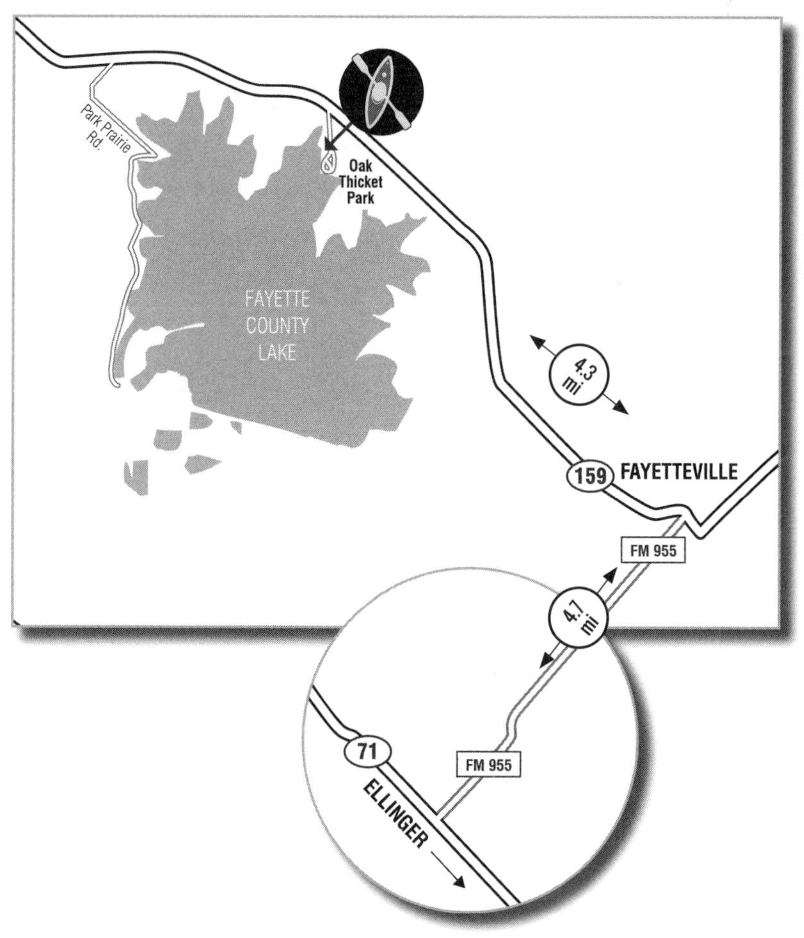

Park Prairie

N 29 56.735, W 96 44.859 Elevation: 396 feet

AT THE INTERSECTION of Texas Highway 71 and FM 955, west of Ellinger, Texas, turn onto FM 955 and travel north 4.7 miles to the intersection of FM 955 and Texas Highway 159 in Fayetteville.

Turn left (west) on Hwy 159 and travel 4.3 miles to the park entrance. Turn left and travel to the boat ramp.

There is a boat ramp sign showing the turn.

There is also a $5 fee for this ramp. Restrooms are available, a pier, and plenty of paved parking.

This park is on the other side of the lake from the Oak Thicket launch.

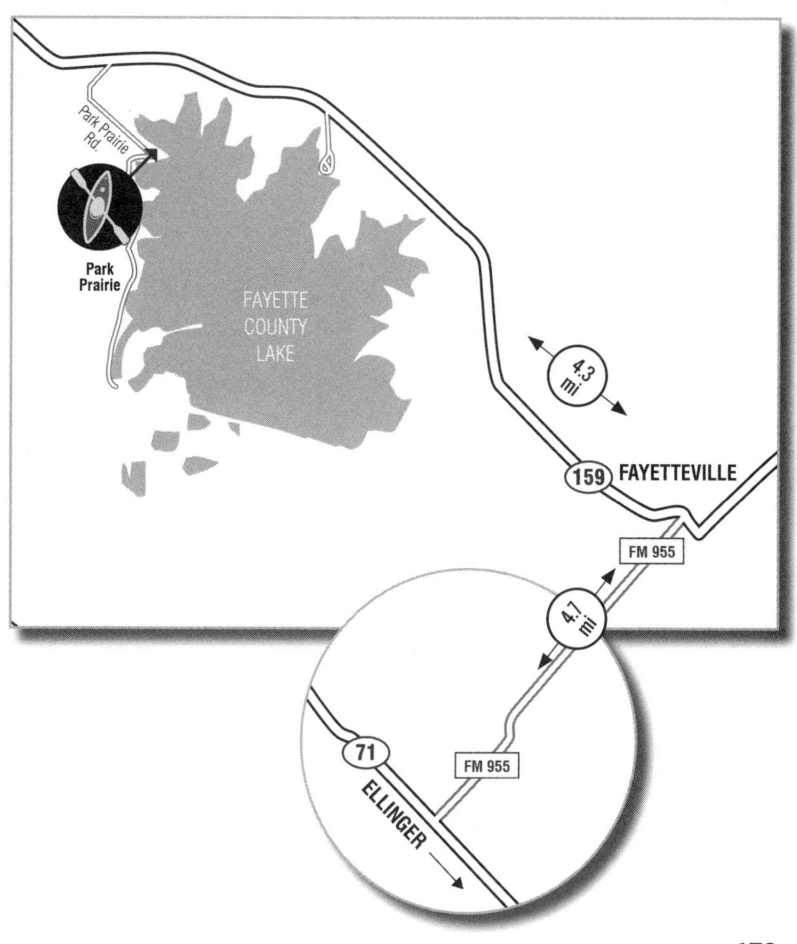

LAKE SOMERVILLE

THERE ARE NINE locations profiled around the shores of Lake Somerville, 18 miles north of Brenham.

Birch Creek State Park	176
Big Creek Park Marina (Private)	178
Overlook Marina (Private)	179
Rocky Creek Park	180
Yegua Creek Park (1)	181
Yegua Creek Park (2)	182
Welch Park	183
Iron Bridge	184
Nails Creek State Park	185

Birch Creek State Park

N 30 18.571, W 96 37.168 Elevation: 249 feet

From the intersection of US 290 and Hwy 36 in Brenham, Texas, continue north on Hwy 36, 15.2 miles. Drive through the town of Somerville north 3.75 miles, to FM 60 in Lyons, Texas. Turn left on FM 60 and travel 6.9 miles to Park Road 57. Turn left on Park Road 57

and travel four miles to the State Park Gate. Entrance fees apply. From the gate turn left and travel 1.5 miles to the ramp. There is plenty of paved parking here, a nice restroom picnic area and fishing pier.

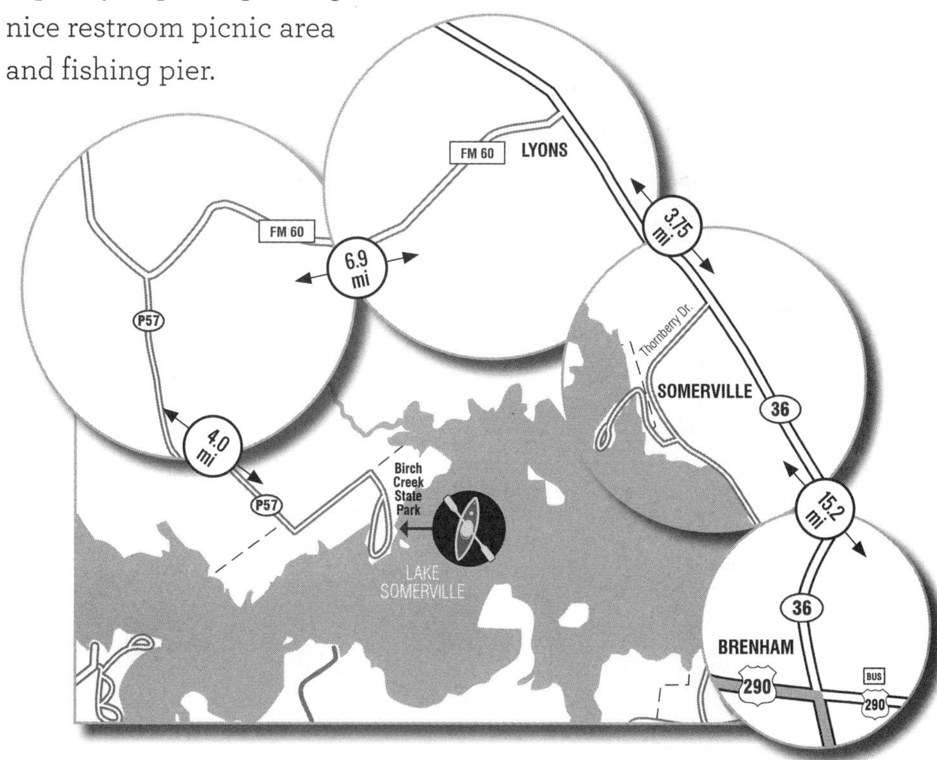

Big Creek Park Marina (Privately Owned)

N 30 19.389, W 96 34.300 Elevation: 241 feet

From the intersection of US 290 and Hwy 36 in Brenham Texas, continue north on Hwy 36, 15.2 miles. Continue through Somerville, 3.75 mi. to FM 60 in Lyons, Texas. Turn left on FM 60 and travel 3.6 miles to R-4. Turn left and travel 3.2 miles to the gate. Travel into the park 1.2 miles to the launch. There is a $5 fee to launch. Restrooms, cabins, a marina and a store are available here.

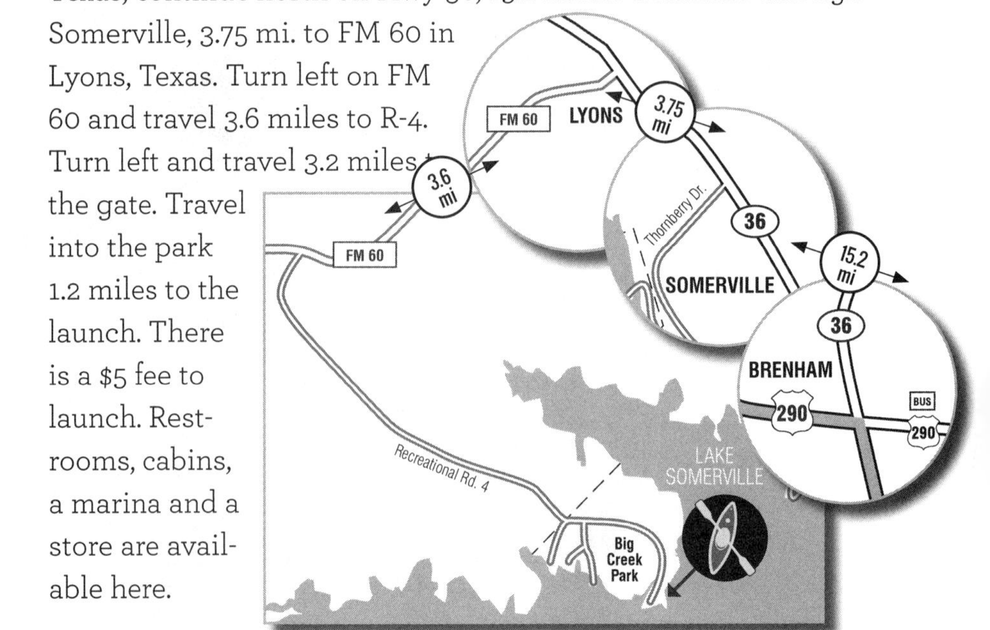

Overlook Marina (Privately Owned)

N 30 18.601, W 96 31.071   Elevation: 247 feet

From the intersection of US 290 and Hwy 36 in Brenham, Texas, continue north on Hwy 36, 11.4 miles. Turn left on FM 1948 for .1 miles, turn right on LBJ drive and travel .5 miles to Marina Dr. Turn left into the gate.

There are two launch points here. One is the marina where they have a store, camping and bait. Fishing off the docks is available. On the other side of the small bay is a paved launch with lots of parking. Both are fee-based launches.

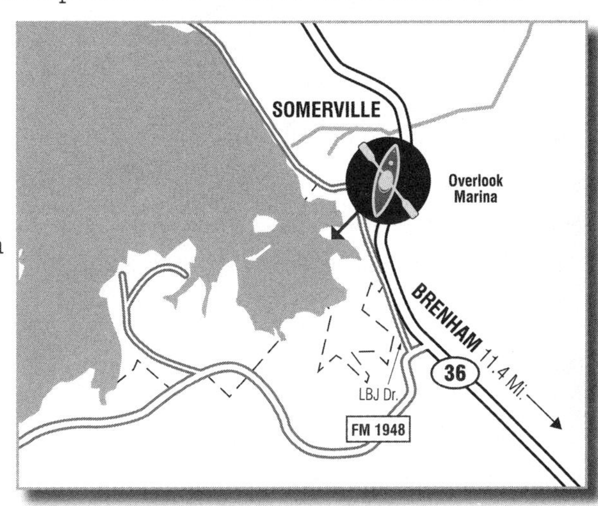

Rocky Creek Park US Army Corps of Engineers

N 30 17.985, W 96 34.352 Elevation: 250 feet

From the intersection of Hwy 36 and FM 1948, (just south of Somerville, Texas), continue west on FM 1948 4.9 miles to the park entrance. There is a big sign showing the entrance. Turn right into the park, and travel .5 miles. The ramp is on the left.

This ramp was closed when I visited Feb 2014, but there is a great sand beach available for kayak launching. There is plenty of paved parking and restrooms available.

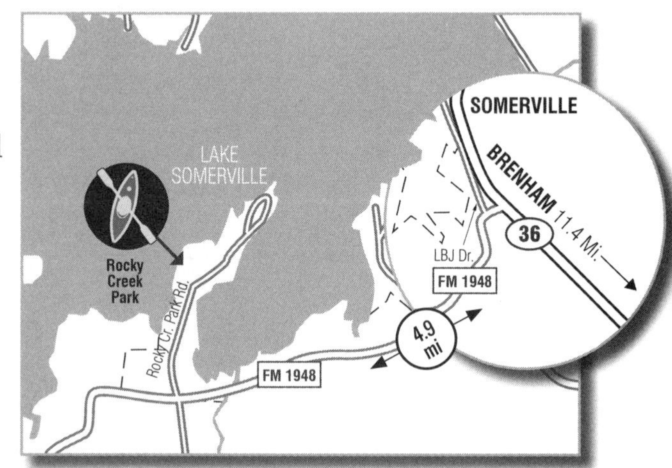

Yegua Creek Park (1)
US Army Corps of Engineers
N 30 18.423, W 96 32.733 Elevation: 245 feet

From the intersection of Hwy 36 and FM 1948, just south of Somerville, Texas, continue west on FM 1948 2.6 miles to the park entrance on the right. After you enter the gate take the first left to ramp #1. This is a paved ramp with plenty of paved parking. No amenities at this ramp.

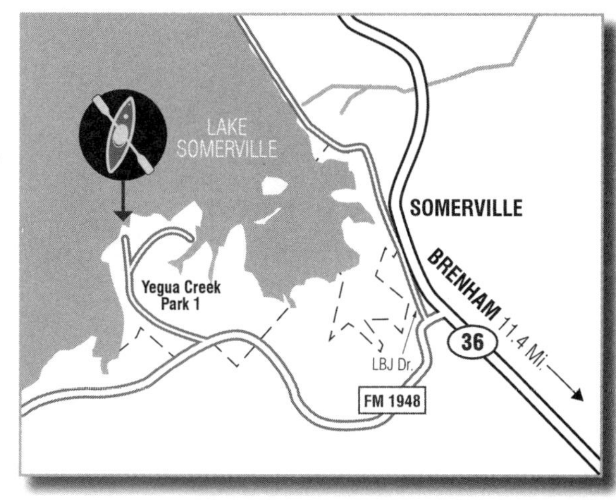

Yegua Creek Park (2)

N 30.3061, W 96.5362 Elevation: 263 feet

From the intersection of Hwy 36 and FM 1948, continue west on FM 1948 2.6 miles to the park entrance. After you enter the gate, continue straight to ramp #2. This is a paved ramp that puts you into a nice protected cove. The restrooms are very close, campsites are nearby and there is a courtesy dock just to the right of the launch. There is plenty of paved parking here.

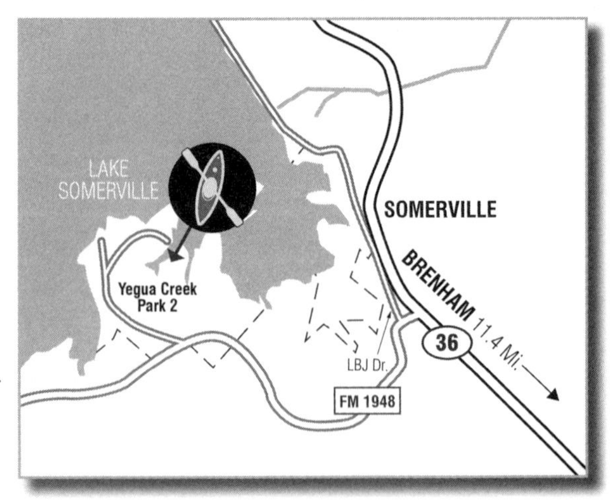

Welch Park

N 30 20.319, W 96 33.019 Elevation: 235 feet

From the intersection of Hwy 36 and Thornberry Ave. in Somerville, Texas, continue east on Thornberry 2.5 miles to the Lake Somerville dam. Turn right at the dam, and follow to the park gate. There is a $2 entry fee. This is a very large park with lots of beach space to launch a kayak. The boat ramp is on a peninsula. There are restrooms, picnic areas and lots of room.

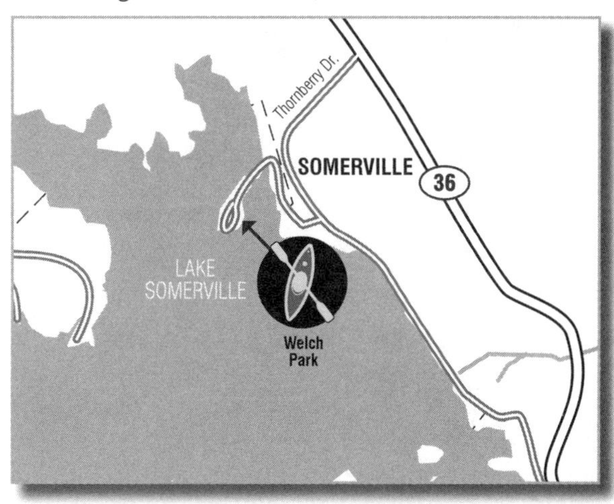

Iron Bridge

N 30 17.703, W 96 37.652 Elevation: 248 feet

From the intersection of FM 1948 and the entrance to Rocky Creek Park, continue west on FM 1948, two miles to CR 594. Turn right on 594 and proceed 2.4 miles to Iron Bridge Rd., and continue straight. This is a gravel road. In 2.1 miles you will arrive at the access point.

This is a remote site that is not on any maps. There are no signs. This is a great launch for kayaks. The iron fence and no formal ramp restrict many boats. There is a nice sand shore. No amenities here.

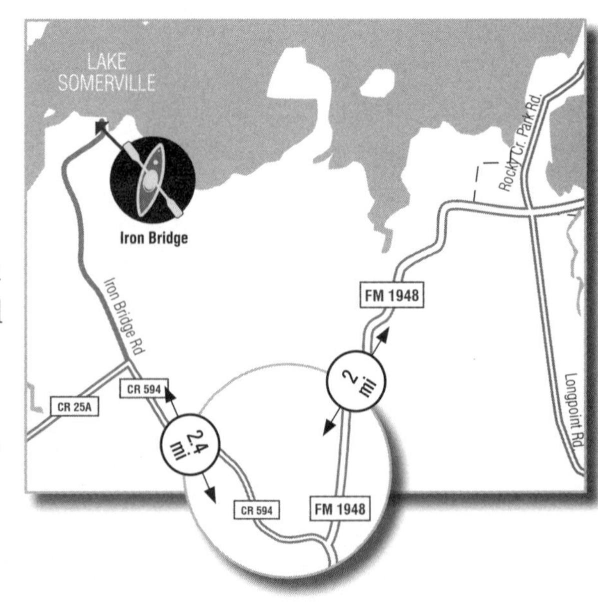

Nails Creek State Park

N 30 17.672, W 96 39.868 Elevation: 249 feet

From the intersection of FM 390 and Hwy 290 in Burton, Texas continue north on FM 390 for one mile and turn left on FM 1697. Continue on FM 1697, 9.5 miles to 180. Turn right, and the entrance to the park is 3.4 miles. The state park has an entry fee, but offers all the amenities, including restrooms with showers, camping, plenty of picnic areas and kayak and canoe rental.

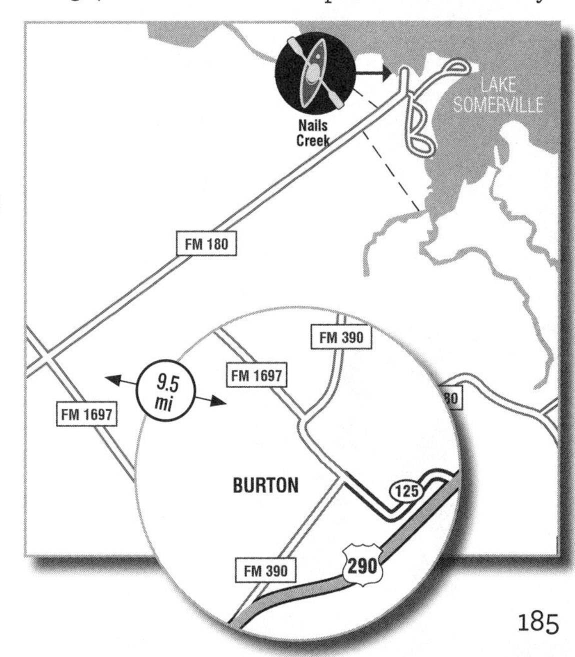

As of this writing, this ramp is closed to all but kayak and canoes until lake levels return to normal.

LAKE LIVINGSTON

LAKE LIVINGSTON, 65 miles northeast of Houston, has eleven launch sites that are profiled here.

Wolf Creek Park	188
Indian Creek Launch	189
Blanchard	190
Tigerville Park	191
Waterfront Lodge	192
Double Lake	193
Point Adventure Bridge	194
356 Marina	195
Cauthin Park	196
Patrick's Ferry	197
Point Blank	197

Wolf Creek Park

N 30 39.727, W 95 08.858 Elevation: 275 feet

From the intersection of US 59 and Hwy 105 in Cleveland, Texas, continue north on Hwy 59 for .5 miles to FM 2025 just north of Cleveland. Turn left and continue 16.7 miles to 150. Turn right 1.5 miles to the town of Coldspring. Turn left on 156 (north) one mile and turn right on FM 224. Travel 6.8 miles to Wolf Creek Park.

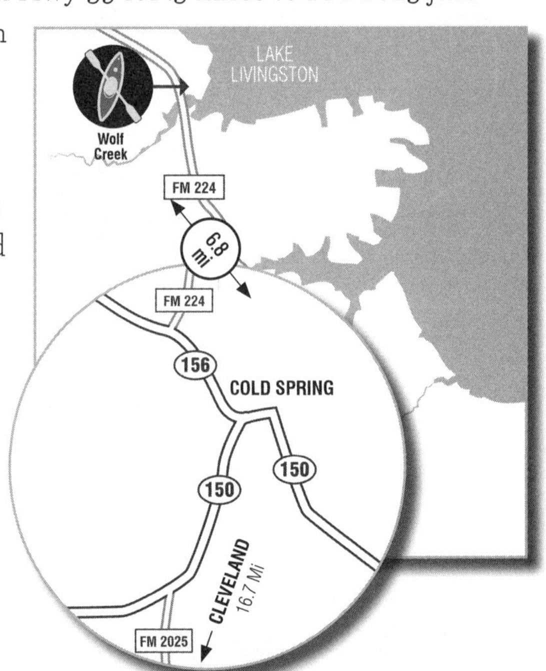

This is a fee launch. The park is a very popular destination and can be very crowded.

Indian Creek Launch

4801 FM 224

N 30.6411, W 95.1403 **Elevation: 134 feet**

From the intersection of US 59 and Hwy 105 in Cleveland, Texas, continue north on Hwy 59 for .5 miles to FM 2025 just north of Cleveland. Turn left and continue 16.7 miles to 150. Turn right 1.5 miles to the town of Coldspring. Turn left on 156 (north), continue one mile and turn right on FM 224. Travel five miles to Indian Creek Store.

This is a one-lane ramp that is off the main body of the lake. Launch fee is required.

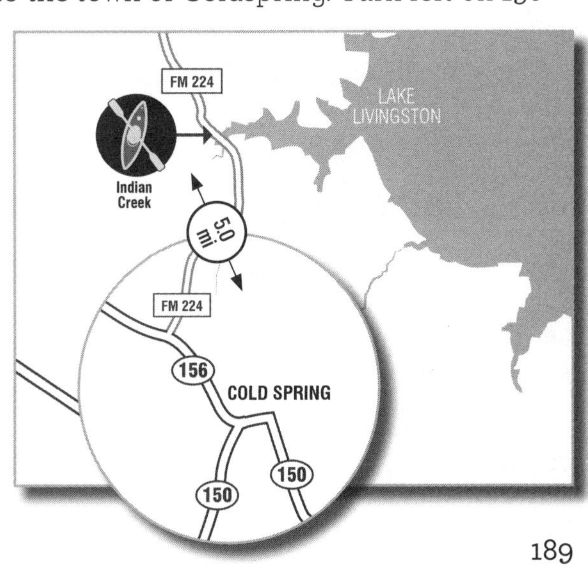

Blanchard

N 30 44.181, W 95 05.387 Elevation: 139 feet

From the intersection of Hwy 190 and US 59 in Livingston, Texas, continue west on Hwy 190 for 4.2 miles to FM 2547. Turn left on FM 2547 and travel 4.7 miles. The road will dead end into the ramp. Can't miss this one—keep driving, and you will hit water. This is a free ramp with two paved lanes. There is plenty of paved parking. No bank fishing allowed, and no amenities are available. This is designed as a launch and retrieve site only.

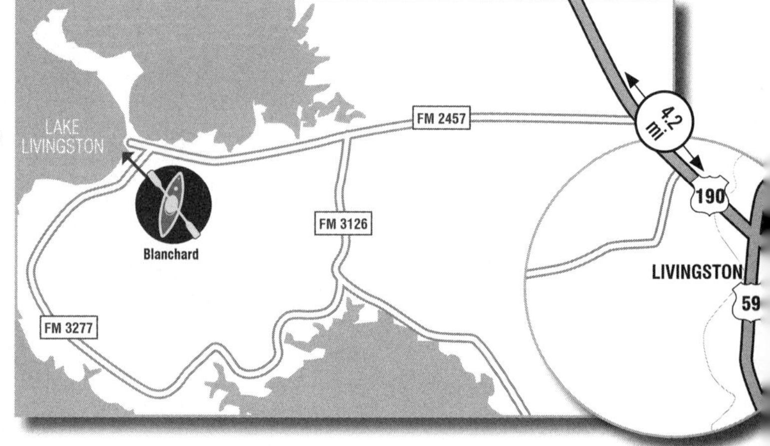

Tigerville Park

N 30 42.920, W 95 03.196 Elevation: 125 feet

From the intersection of Hwy 190 and US 59 in Livingston, Texas, continue west on Hwy 190 4.2 miles to FM 2547. Turn left on FM 2547 and travel 2.6 miles to FM 3126. Turn left on FM 3126 and continue 1.5 miles. The park is on your right. There is no sign on the road and only a small sign in the park. The launch is free. It has a nice paved, one-lane ramp and access to a small cove. There is a restroom, picnic area and a small pier.

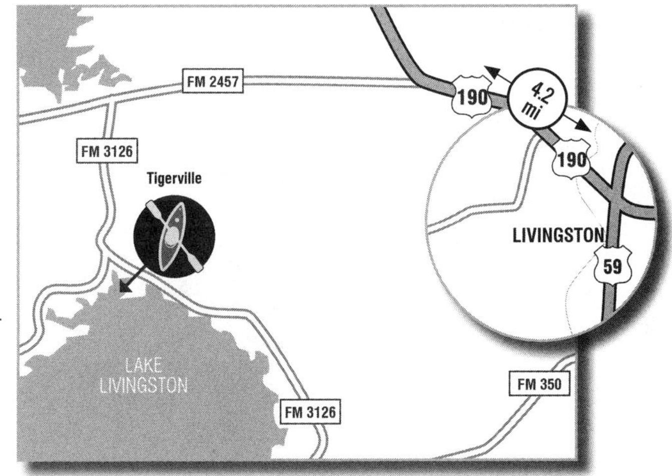

Waterfront Lodge

371 Navaho Trail

N 30 48.696, W 95 05.766 Elevation: 147 feet

FROM THE INTERSECTION of Hwy 190 and Navaho Trail, continue south on Navaho for .3 miles to the lake. There is a $5 launch fee if you are not staying at the lodge. They have all the amenities available re. This includes a store, lodging, RV park and a marina. In the RV park, there is a small ramp, which is well-suited for kayaks.

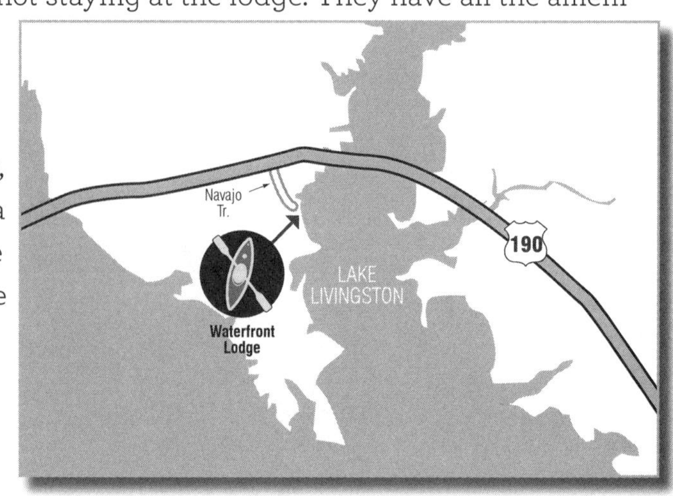

Double Lake

301 FM 2025

N 30 32.861, W 95 07.974 Elevation: 286 feet

From the intersection of US 59 and Bus. Hwy 105 in Cleveland, Texas, continue north on US 59 for 1.3 miles to FM 2025 just north of Cleveland. Turn left and continue 16 miles. The entrance to Double Lake will be on your right. This is a fee park. The water levels have been down in this park over the past year, so it may not be accessible. Check with the forest service before you go.

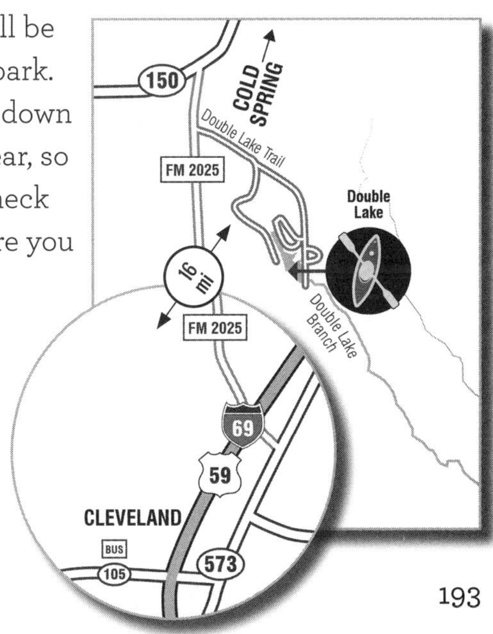

Double Lake Recreation Area: (936) 344-6205.

This is a very nice protected water that did hold some nice fish in the past.

Point Adventure Bridge

N 30 54.023, W 95 13.647 Elevation: 127 feet

From the intersection of FM 356 and Hwy 190 In Onalaska, Texas, continue north on 365 for 9.8 miles to this bridge. Parking is available beside the bridge. This is not a formal launch site. No amenities available here.

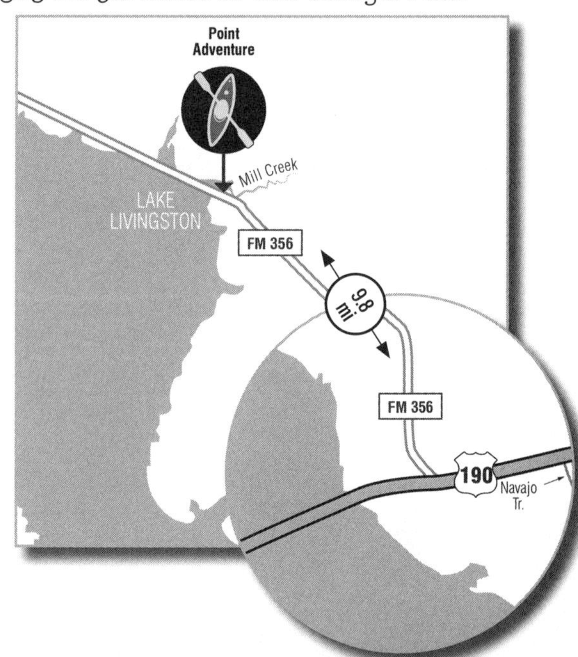

356 Marina

N 30 54.750, W 95 15.764   Elevation: 142 feet

From the intersection of Hwy 190 and FM 356 in Onalaska, Texas, continue north on 356 for 12.1 miles. The launch will be on your right before the bridge.

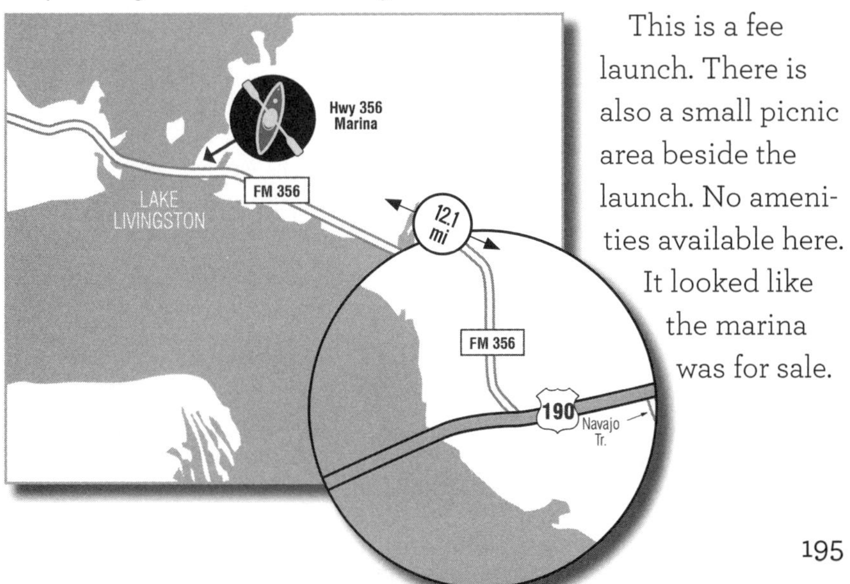

This is a fee launch. There is also a small picnic area beside the launch. No amenities available here. It looked like the marina was for sale.

Cauthin Park

N 30 58.096, W 95 19.983 Elevation: 137 feet

FROM THE INTERSECTION of FM 356 and Hwy 94 in Trinity, Texas, continue east on Hwy 94 for 2.7 miles.

As soon as you cross the bridge the access will be on your right. There is a public boat ramp sign. This is a free ramp that is on White Rock Creek and feeds the lake. There is a sand bank under the bridge that you can also launch from. No amenities here.

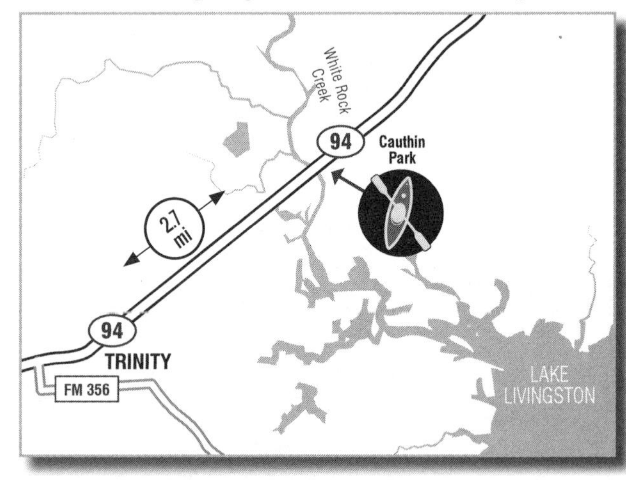

Patrick's Ferry

N 30 47.850, W 95 09.627 Elevation: 118 feet

THIS LAUNCH IS located on the west side of Lake Livingston on Hwy 190 Bridge. This is a free launch. There is plenty of paved parking, and a sand bank suitable for a kayak launch is on the right side of the ramp. It's very easy to find and access the lake. No amenities are available here.

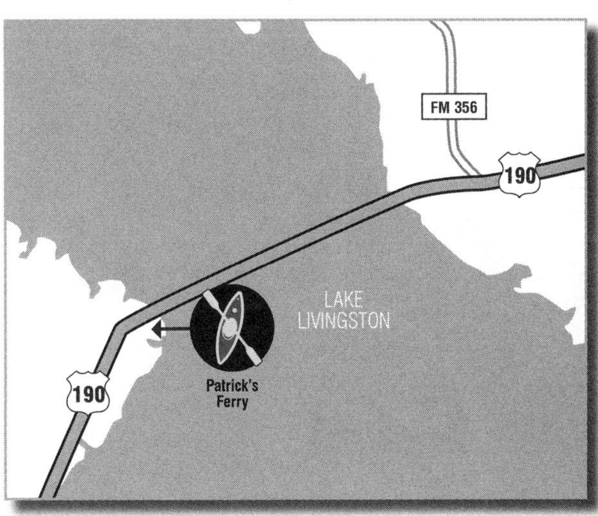

Point Blank

N 30 44.755, W 95 12.447 Elevation: 132 feet

From the west side of the Hwy 190 Bridge, on Lake Livingston continue west five miles, to Point Blank, Texas, and turn left on 156. Continue on 156 for .5 miles, 156 will make a right, 90-degree turn, and you will want to stay straight another .3 miles to get to the launch. There is a flashing yellow light where 156 turns. This is a free, paved, one-lane launch. On the side of the ramp there is also a sand bank suitable for a kayak.

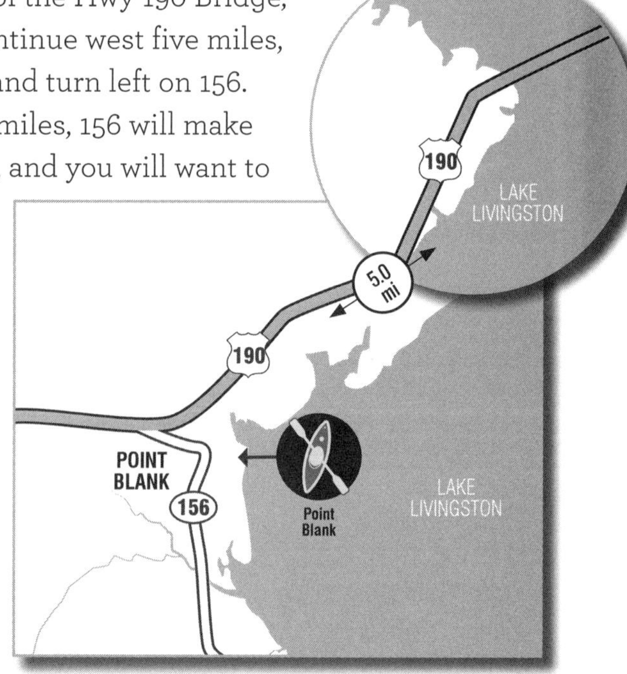

SPRING & CYPRESS CREEKS

SPRING AND CYPRESS Creeks are located in northern Harris County, between Houston and Conroe.

There are eight launch sites profiled on these creeks.

Collins Park	202
Kuykendahl	204
Pundt Park	206
Riley Fuzzel	208
Carter Park	209
Cypresswood Drive Bridge	210
Jesse Jones Park & Nature Center	211
Edgewater San Jacinto River	212

Spring- Cypress Creeks

PCT 4 OPERATES four launches on Spring and Cypress Creeks. Collins Park, Pundt Park, Carter Park and Jesse Jones Park. In order to use these launches you must follow the rules and regulations. This includes submitting forms with information about your trip. Here are the basic rules.

PRECINCT 4 CANOEING/KAYAKING Rules and Regulations

PRECINCT 4 OFFERS launches at Collins Park, Jesse H. Jones Park & Nature Center, and Pundt Park for those interested in canoeing/kayaking Spring or Cypress Creeks and associated waterways. Please review the following information and submit a completed Canoeing/Kayaking Reservation Form prior to using a launch at a Harris County Precinct 4 location.

Notice must be given to the Harris County Precinct 4 launch and/or retrieval location at least 24 hours in advance of a launch for weekday trips. Weekend reservations must be submitted by 3 p.m. on Friday.

Canoes/kayaks may not be launched and retrieved from the same location. Please contact Precinct 4 facilities for specific availability/access information.

Visitors should be aware of the water conditions on their planned date and route.

All participants are required to adhere to Texas Parks & Wildlife watercraft regulations regarding boating and personal flotation device requirements. For more information, visit www.tpwd.state.tx.us/fishboat/boat/safety/life_jackets. Harris County Precinct 4 facilities do not rent canoes/kayaks.

Note: Water levels of the creeks affect the trip times.

APPROXIMATE TRIP DURATIONS:

- Collins Park* to the Kuykendahl Road, launch at Cypress Creek on the southeast side of the bridge (3.5 miles)
- Kuykendahl Road, launch at Cypress Creek (on the south-east side of the bridge) to Cypresswood Drive bridge between Treaschwig and FM 1960 (11.6 miles)
- Cypresswood Drive bridge (between Treaschwig and FM 1960) to Jones Park*: four hours
- Jones Park* to Edgewater Park (at Hwy. 59 and Hamblen Road): two hours
- Pundt Park* to Jones Park*: six hours
- Riley-Fuzzel Preserve (Montgomery County) to Jones Park*: eight hours

(Facilities maintained by Harris County Precinct 4 are marked with an asterisk (*). All others are operated by separate entities.)

Vehicles remaining at a Harris County Precinct 4 location after hours are subject to towing at the owner's expense.

Completed reservation forms and advance notice of canoe/kayak trips are processed at Jones Park, Pundt Park, and the Parks Reservations Office Monday through Friday from 8 a.m. to 3 p.m.

Note: Precinct 4 parks are open every day of the year except Thanksgiving, Christmas Eve, Christmas Day, and New Year's Day.

PRECINCT 4 PARKS DEPARTMENT
22540 ALDINE WESTFIELD ROAD
SPRING, TX 77373 281.353.8100
www.hcp4.net

Collins Park

6727 Cypresswood Drive, Spring, Texas 77379

N 30 00.594, W 95 30.593 Elevation: 104 feet

For reservations, call 281.353.4196 Monday through Friday from 8 a.m. to 3 p.m. Hours of Operation Monday-Friday: 7 a.m. to 10 p.m. Saturday and Sunday: 8 a.m. to 10 p.m.

From the intersection of Hwy 249 and Cypresswood Dr., continue east on Cypresswood four miles to N Greenfield Drive.

Turn right on N Greenfield .1 miles to the park gate. There is no fee for entry to this park. There is no formal launch site here. There is bank access to Cypress Creek, but it's a fairly steep walk down to the creek. The park has lots of options—hiking, biking, playgrounds and basketball. Restrooms are available.

Collins Park* to the Kuykendahl Road, launch at Cypress Creek on the southeast side of the bridge, estimated (3.5 miles)

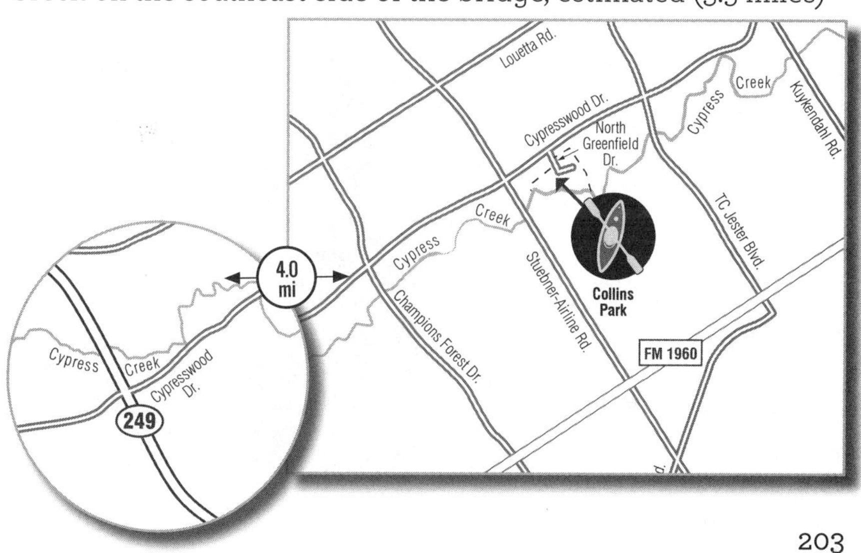

Kuykendahl

17207 Kuykendahl

N 30 01.457, W 95 28.562 Elevation: 121 feet

From the intersection of Cypresswood Dr. and Kuykendahl, continue south on Kuykendahl .1 miles to the bridge. Access is a gravel road on the left that goes beside the street and under the bridge. It can be very muddy in wet weather

This is not a formal park or launch site. Although it is listed as a launch/takeout, there are no signs or

amenities. There are access points on both the north side and south side of the bridge. On the south side there is a no trespass and no motor vehicle sign—along a very well-used road. I would stick to the north side of the bridge. There are no signs, but a couple of spots look much easier to launch from. Access to the creek will be down a steep bank. There is a very large culvert with a landing on the right side that looked to be the best spot to put in.

From Kuykendahl Road, launch at Cypress Creek (on the southeast side of the bridge) to Cypresswood Drive bridge between Treaschwig and FM 1960 (estimated) 11.6 miles.

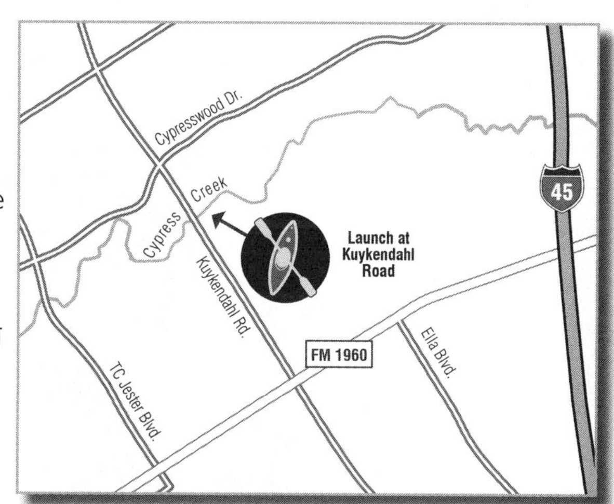

Pundt Park

4129 Spring Creek Drive, Spring, Texas 77373

N 30 04.907, W 95 22.720 Elevation: 58 feet

For reservations, call 281.353.4196 Monday through Friday from 8 a.m. to 3 p.m., or 832.527.7436 after hours and during weekends. Hours of Operation 8 a.m. to dusk.

From the intersection of Aldine Westfield and Louetta Rd., continue south on Aldine Westfield, .5 miles and turn left on Spring Creek Dr.(before you get to Cypresswood Dr.)

Travel on Spring Creek Dr. 1.7 miles to the park entrance. Continue on the main park road past the playground and restrooms. You will come to a circular drive that is labeled "trailer turn around." Continue straight through. It looks like you are going onto a trail into the wood, and you are. This is the loop to get you to the creek and drop off your boat.

You cannot park there, but you can enter and unload. You will travel back out to park in a field parking lot.

The launch is 100 yards from the vehicle drop off. A nice sand bank on the creek should make it very easy.

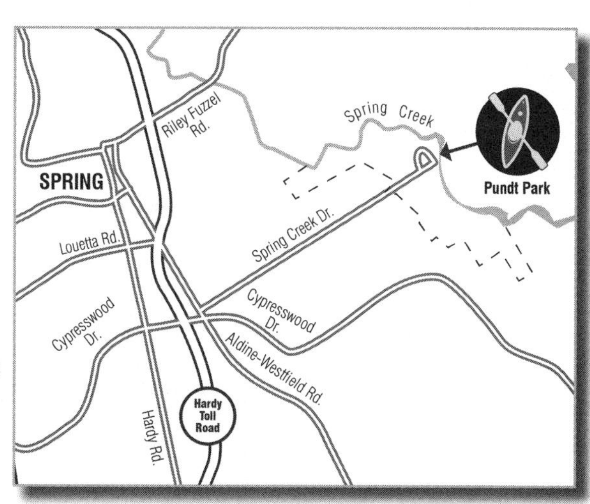

Pundt Park* to Jones Park*: six hours (all float times are estimates.)

Riley Fuzzel Preserve

N 30 05.530, W 95 24.328 Elevation: 69 feet

From the intersection of the Hardy Toll Road and 1960, travel north on the Hardy Toll Road 8. 5 miles to the Riley Fuzzel exit.

Exit and turn right, continue on Riley Fuzzel .5 miles. Cross the creek bridge and take your next left onto Old Riley Fuzzel Rd. No amenities here.

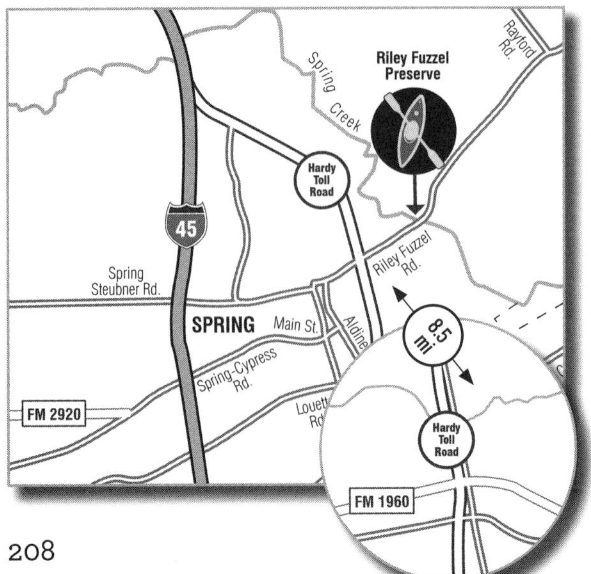

Riley Fuzzel Preserve (Montgomery County) to Jones Park: eight hours (all float times are estimates.)

Carter Park

N 30 03.163, W 95 19.582   Elevation: 68 feet

From the intersection of Treaschwig and Cypresswood Dr., continue east on Treaschwig 1.5 miles to the entrance of the park. This launch is behind locked gates so you will need to make reservations with Pct 4 to be able to access the creek. 281-353-4196. The access will allow you to drive within 75 yards of the creek. There is a nice sand bank to launch from or take out. This is a good middle spot between Pundt Park 4.2 miles upstream and Jesse Jones Park 3.4 miles downstream. No amenities here. One porta can. There is a very nice covered (shooting area) archery range open to the public in this park.

Cypresswood Drive Bridge

N 30 01.793, W 95 19.809 Elevation: 38 feet

From the intersection of FM 1960 and Cypresswood drive, west of Humble, Texas continue north on Cypresswood .9 miles and exit right to the U-turn under the bridge.

There is no formal ramp here and no signs marking this launch. There is very limited parking under the bridge. It is a short 50-yard walk down the hill to access the creek. There is a nice sand bank to launch from when the creek is flowing under normal conditions.

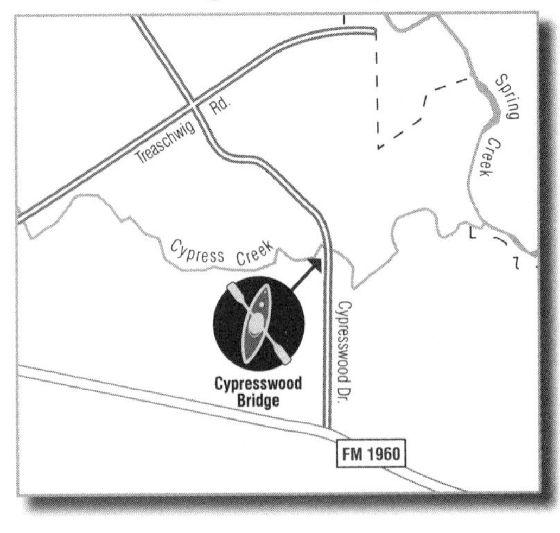

No amenities here.

Jesse H. Jones Park & Nature Center

20634 Kenswick Drive, Humble, Texas 77338

N 30 01.399, W 95 17.644 Elevation: 47 feet

FROM THE INTERSECTION of FM 1960 and Kenswick Dr., continue north on Kenswick one mile to the park entrance. The launch is about ½ mile from the park entrance. The park will have to unlock a gate for you to travel back to the creek. You will be allowed to go in and drop off or pick up only.

No parking is allowed at the launch site. Jones Park has many activities and some great hiking trails. Restrooms are available.

Jones Park* to Edgewater Park (at Hwy. 59 and Hamblen Road): two hours (all float times are estimates.)

Phone: 281.446.8588

E-mail: jjp@hcp4.net

Hours of Operation: Entrance gate closes 30 minutes prior to park closing. 8 a.m. to dusk

Nature Center is open daily from 8 a.m. to 4:30 p.m.

Edgewater/San Jacinto River

N 30 01.641, W 95 15.306 Elevation: 1 foot

From the intersection of FM 1960 and Hwy 59 in Humble, Texas travel north on 59 and exit Townsend Blvd. Continue on the feeder 1.5 miles, and turn right on Hamblen Road. Travel .1 miles and turn right on the dirt road before you get to the railroad tracks.

There is a mailbox there with 220 Hamblen on it. Continue .3 miles to the entrance.

There is a $5 launch fee. This launch will put you into the San Jacinto River south of Spring Creek.

Under normal flow you will be able to paddle upstream to the confluence with Spring Creek, or downstream eventually to Lake Houston. They have done some work on the road from Hamblen to the launch, making it much better. No amenities here.

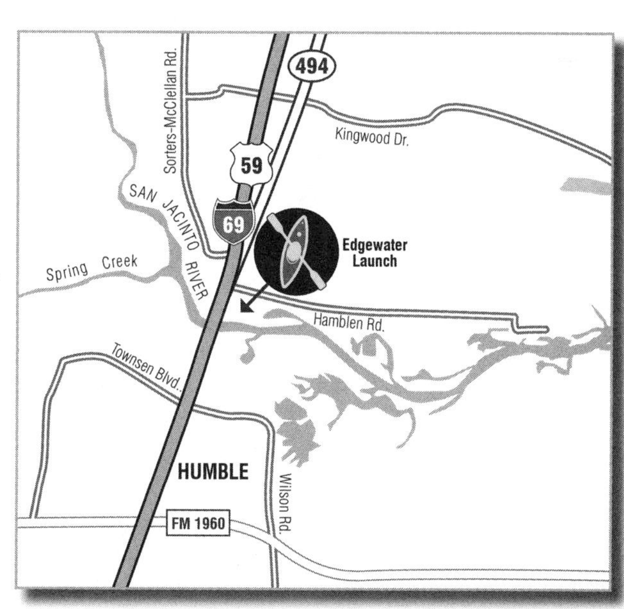

BRAZOS RIVER SIMONTON

SIMONTON IS 21.5 miles west of Hwy 6 in Houston on FM 1093 (Westheimer Rd.).

Two launch sites on the Brazos River are profiled.

1093 Launch 216

FM 1489 Mullins Crossing 218

FM 1093 Launch

N 29 40.375, W 96 01.195 Elevation: 96 feet

From the intersection of FM 1093 and FM 1489 in Simonton, Texas, continue west on 1093, 2.5 miles. Turn right before you cross the river, and the ramp is under the bridge.

There is a canoe launch sign here. I would not consider this an improved ramp. When I was there it was pretty muddy along the "road"—4WD muddy.

There is a place to park that is high and dry, but you will have to portage your boat 150-200 yards to get to the river. If it is dry you may be able to make it with a 2WD truck. There is no real ramp, just a dirt trail down to the river. When the river is at normal levels there are plenty of spots to launch from. There was a lot of wood debris collected on the bridge supports.

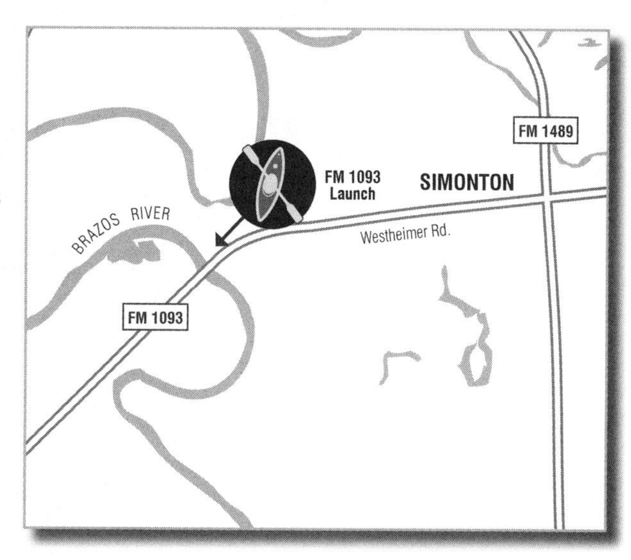

FM 1489 Mullins Crossing

N 29 38.423, W 95 58.563 Elevation: 101 feet

From the intersection of FM 1093 and FM 1489 in Simonton, Texas, continue south on FM 1489, 2.4 miles. The launch is on the right before you cross the river bridge. There is a canoe launch sign at the highway. This launch spot is very steep and very narrow. If it is wet, this will be a challenge to get your boat to/from the water. I do not see how you would get more than one boat at a time

down the narrow trail to the water. I would suggest you review the pictures before you attempt to launch. It is not an improved site, just a steep trail to the river. There is not much room to access the water.

Fishing the Brazos can be very rewarding. Try to find some deeper holes for catfish. Plenty of brush and structure, will make great habitat for pan-fish and bass. Gar is also a big target species in this river.

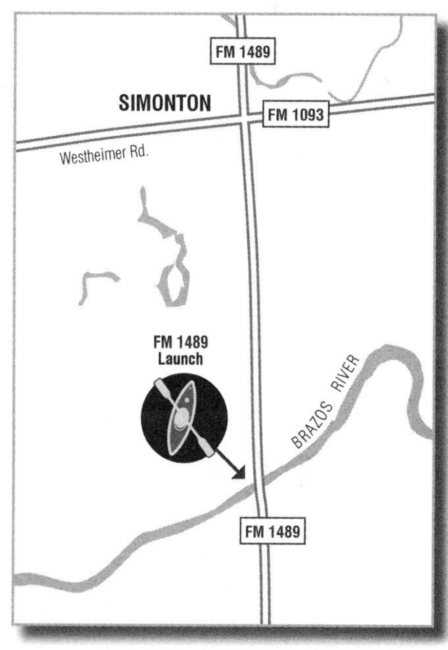

LAKE TEXANA

LAKE TEXANA IS situated 90 miles southwest of Houston on U.S. Highway 59, between the communities of Ganado and Edna.

The lake has six launch sites that are profiled here.

Hwy 172 Launch 222

County Road 237 Launch 223

Hwy 111 Launch 224

Breckenridge Complex Ramp 7 225

Hwy 59 Ramp 4 226

Hwy 59 Ramp 3 227

Hwy 172 Launch

N 29 01.549, W 96 30.395 Elevation: 32 feet

FROM THE INTERSECTION of Hwy 59 and 172 in Ganado, Texas, continue east on 172 for 1.8 miles. The lake access will be on your right before you cross the bridge. No amenities here, but this is a free launch site. The lake is still very low, but this north end has plenty of fishable water.

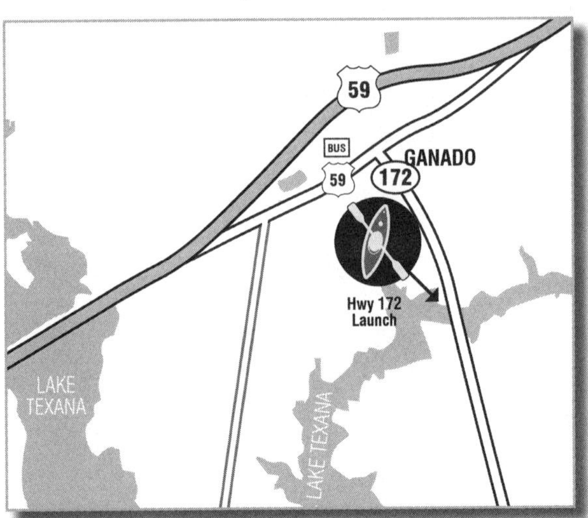

237 Launch

N 28 58.380, W 96 31.494 Elevation: 31 feet

FROM THE INTERSECTION of Hwy 59 and 172 in Ganado, Texas, continue east on 172 for 5.5 miles, to CR 237. Turn right on 237 and the road will dead end at the lake access in two miles. No amenities here. A very nice gravel ramp puts you in just north of the 111 bridge.

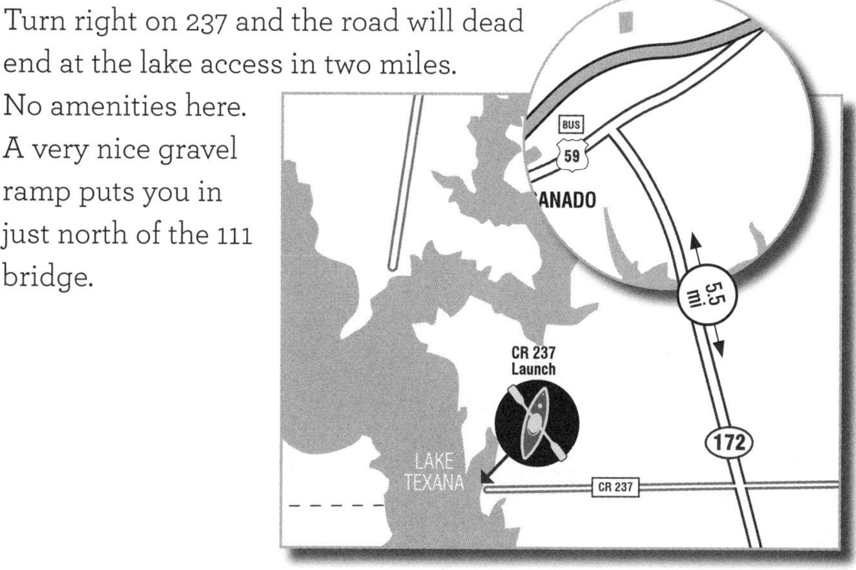

Hwy 111 Launch

N 28 57.209, W 96 32.328 Elevation: 22 feet

From the intersection of Hwy 59 and 111 in Edna, Texas, continue east on 111, 3.3 miles. The park is on the right. This access is at the bridge on the west side of the lake. There is no formal launch here. You can access the water along the shoreline. This is the day-use area of Breckenridge Park. This section of the park has covered picnic tables. No other amenities.

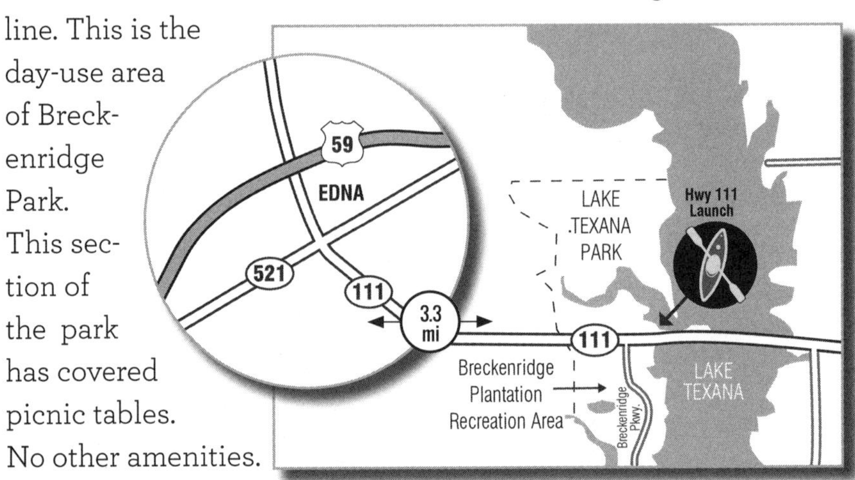

Breckenridge Complex Ramp 7

N 28 56.197, W 96 32.593 Elevation: 29 feet

From the intersection of Hwy 59 and 111 in Edna, Texas, continue east on 111, 3.1 miles. The park is on the right. This is a large park complex with all the amenities. The public ramp is located within the park by the gazebo.

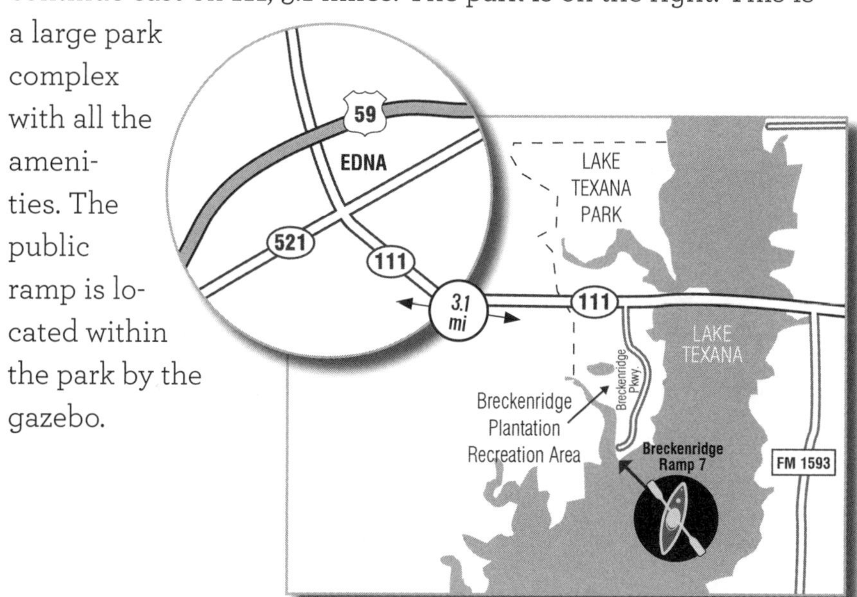

Hwy 59 Ramp 4

N 29 01.309, W 96 34.176 Elevation: 34 feet

From the town of Ganado on Hwy 59 continue south on Hwy 59, 4 miles across the bridge and turn right into the park. No amenities available here.

This is a paved ramp that is free, with bank access. It is off the main body of the lake, and it provides some wind protection for kayakers. There is a sign on the highway showing this ramp location.

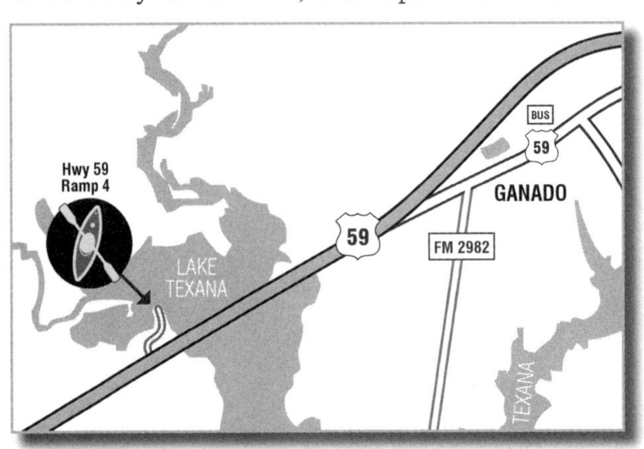

Hwy 59 Ramp 3

N 1 30.910, W 96 32.950   Elevation: 39 feet

From the town of Ganado on Hwy 59 continue south three miles. This ramp is on the north side of the bridge before you cross this section of the lake. Turn left to access the lake.

There is a public boat ramp sign on the highway. No amenities available here, but plenty of paved parking. This location is right along the side of Hwy 59.

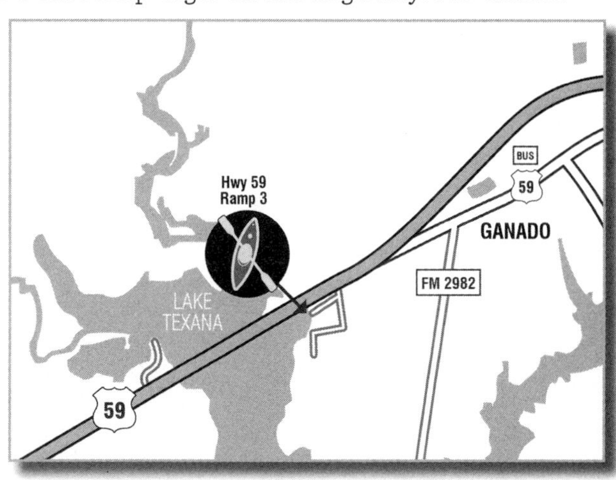

VICTORIA

THERE ARE TWO public launches with access to the Guadalupe River, both located in the city limits of Victoria, Texas.

Riverside Park is a large city park on the west side of Victoria. It is home to the zoo and public golf course, so there are plenty of signs directing you here from every main street.

Riverside Boat Ramp 230

Pumphouse 231

Riverside Boat Ramp

N 28 49.481, W 97 00.925   Elevation: 75 feet

From the intersection of Red River Drive and Memorial at the entrance to Riverside Park, turn right and continue straight for 1.4 miles. Memorial will become McCright Drive. The ramp entrance will be on your left. There are no amenities at the ramp but, restrooms are available within the park. The launch is a one-lane paved ramp with a small dock beside it.

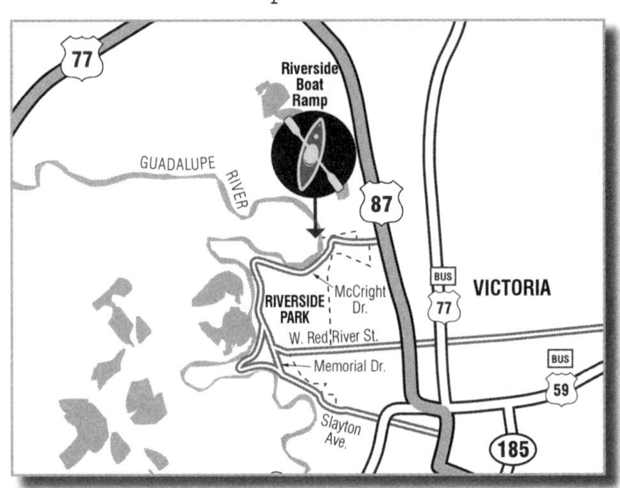

This is designed as the put-in spot, but under normal flow you could paddle either way.

Pumphouse

1201 Stayton Ave.

N 28 48.368, W 97 00.960   Elevation: 82 feet

From the intersection of Red River Drive and Memorial at the entrance to Riverside Park, turn left on Memorial, .2 miles then left on Memorial/McCright past the zoo, a total of .6 miles. The Pumphouse Restaurant is the site of this access.

The walkway to the river is on the left side of the restaurant parking lot. There is limited parking here. You will need to portage about 150 yards on a nice paved trail then down some steep metal stairs to a floating dock. This spot is designed as a take-out point, with the put-in being Riverside Boat Ramp. No amenities available at this site.

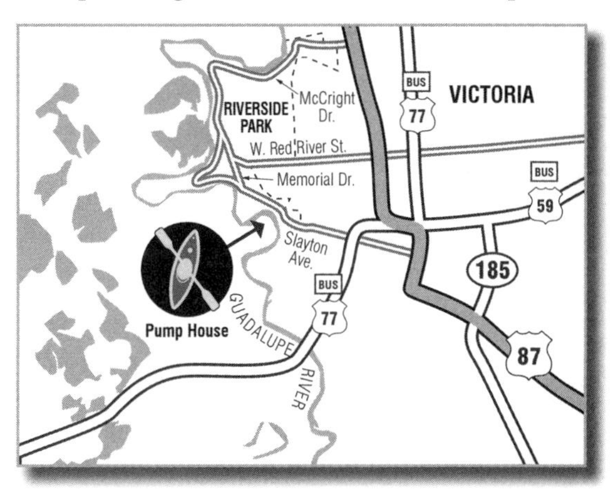

GUADALUPE RIVER

THIS AREA AROUND Seguin, Texas has two free public launches, and one privately owned, fee-based launch with access to the Guadalupe River.

The Guadalupe is generally a controlled flow and will offer some protection from wind. Fish species you can expect will include Guadalupe (spotted) bass, catfish and crappie.

Max Starcke Park 234

Lake Placid (I-10) 235

Rivershade RV Park 236

Max Starcke Park

N 29 33.091, W 97 58.236 Elevation: 486 feet

From the intersection of I -10 and State Hwy 123 Business continue south on Hwy 123 Business 3.4 mi., until you reach Max Starcke park.

You will exit right onto River Dr. and proceed straight to the launch. It is a concrete bulkhead with stairs that allow you water access. No fee required.

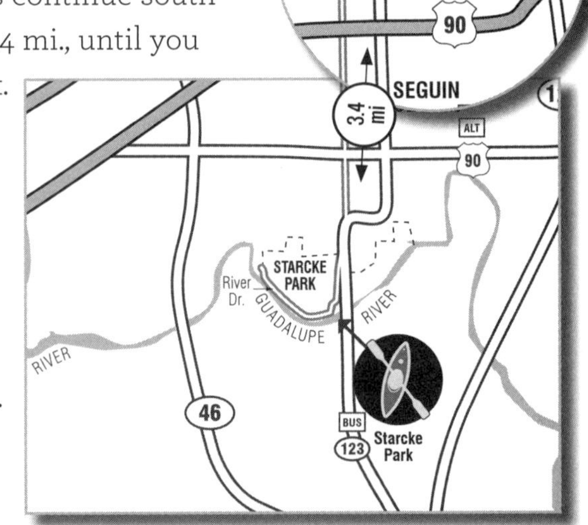

Lake Placid (I-10)

N 30 34.236, W 98 01.379 Elevation: 355 feet

From I-10, continue 2.5 miles west of Seguin, Texas and take the FM 494 exit (Exit# 605). Go right on FM 494, then take a right on Quintana Rd.. and follow this until you are under the bridge. This area has been under construction so you may have to work around barrels.

There is a public boat ramp sign here. This is a single-lane, paved ramp under the bridge. No amenities are available here. No fee required. This ramp is open all year.

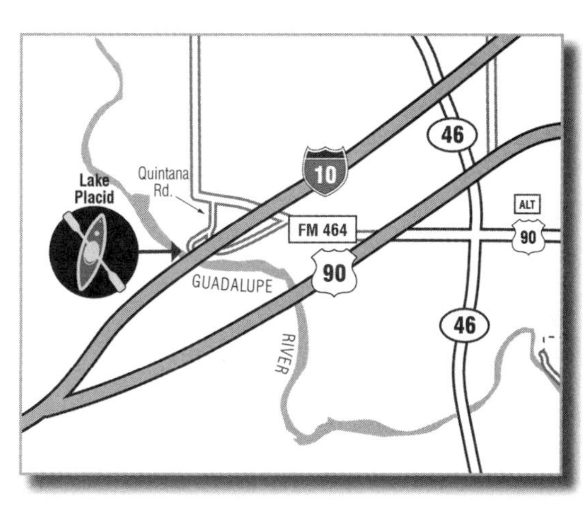

Rivershade RV Park

3993 S. 123 Bypass, Seguin, Texas
N 29 32.789, W 97 57.012
Elevation: 477 feet

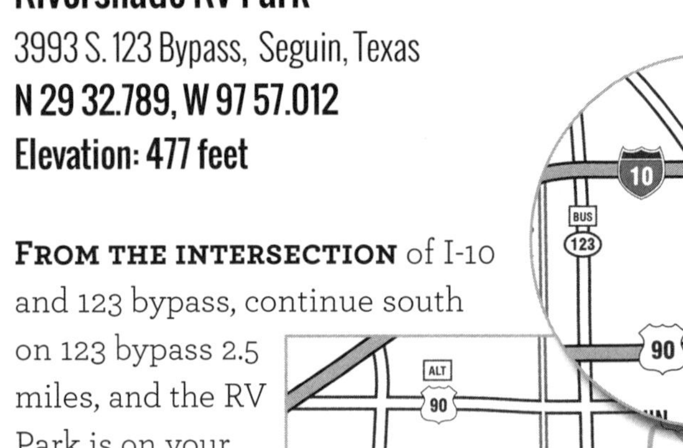

From the intersection of I-10 and 123 bypass, continue south on 123 bypass 2.5 miles, and the RV Park is on your left. This is a fee launch and is located within the RV Park.

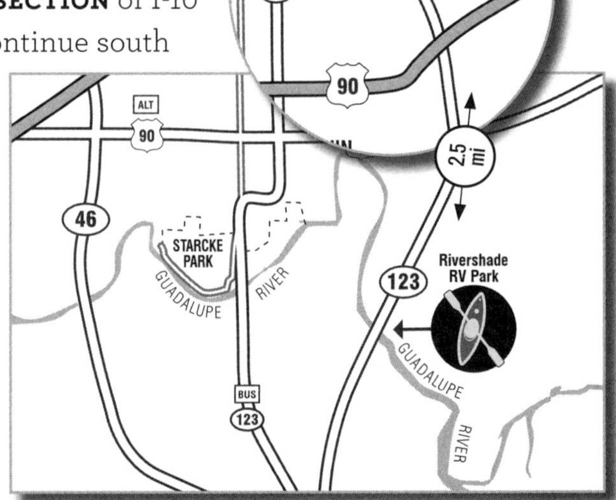

GOLIAD

THREE LAUNCH SITES are profiled in the Goliad area, a community situated at the intersection of U.S. Highways 59 and 183 on the banks of the San Antonio River.

San Antonio River at Hwy 59 238

Ferry Street 239

Goliad State Park 240

San Antonio River at Hwy 59

N 28 39.111, W 97 25.935 Elevation: 120 feet

From the intersection of Hwy 183 and Hwy 59 in Goliad, Texas, continue west on Hwy 59, 2.9 miles. The access is on the right before you cross the bridge. There is a paddle trail sign here. A set of metal stairs gets you to the river edge.

There is also bank access here to launch from. Plenty of parking is available and one porta-can. This is a free launch site.

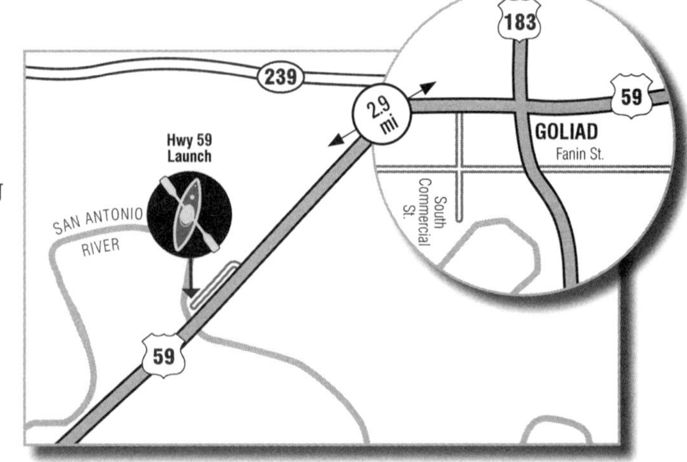

Ferry Street

N 28 39.644, W 97 23.549 Elevation: 125 feet

From the intersection of Hwy 183 and Hwy 59 in Goliad Texas, continue west on Hwy 59, .2 miles. Turn left on S. Commercial St. this will dead end into the parking lot.

Access to the river is about 100 yards from here, Metal stairs lead to bank access to launch from. No amenities are available here.

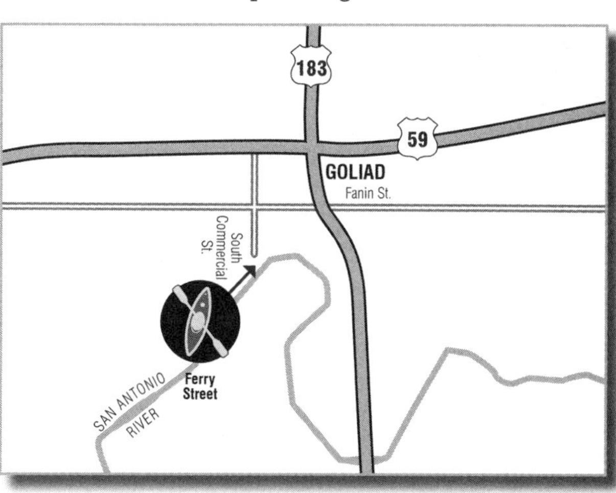

This is a free public launch.

Goliad State Park

N 28 39.157, W 97 22.966 Elevation: 85 feet

From the intersection of Hwy 183 and Hwy 59 in Goliad, Texas, continue south on Hwy 183 for .9 miles. The state park entrance is on your right. Entry fee required.

Stay to the left when you enter the park and continue .8 miles to the river access point. You will need to portage about 150 yards.

The dock here was above the water line, so the bank just to the left offered the best spot to launch from. This location is designed as a take-out for the above two launch points.

The state park has all the amenities including restrooms, showers, and lots of history.

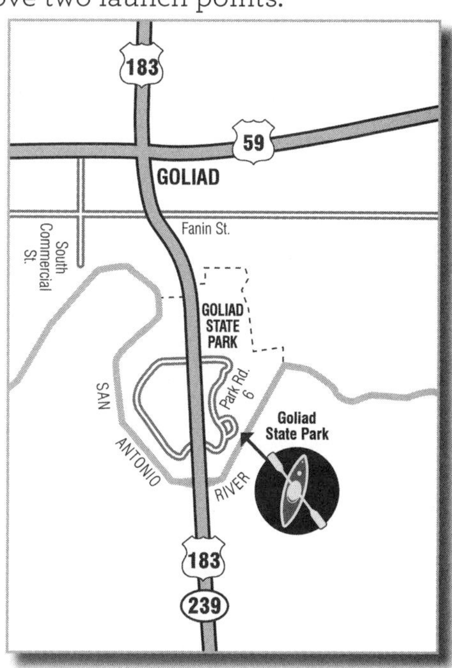

BOERNE AND COLETO CREEK

THE LAST TWO sites profiled Boerne, located 32 miles northwest of San Antoino off I-10 , and on Coleto Creek Reservoir, a power plant cooling lake located off U.S. Highway 59 just south of Victoria.

Boerne City Lake	244
Coleto Creek	246

Boerne City Lake

N 29 49.622, W 98 46.223 Elevation: 1,522 feet

FROM THE INTERSECTION of I-10 and Hwy 46, in Boerne, Texas, continue west on I-10 2.8 miles to the Ranger Creek exit. Exit, turn left under the bridge and take an immediate right on the access road. (It's two-way traffic.) Travel 3.4 miles to Upper Cibolo Creek Rd. and turn left. Continue .6 miles, and the park entrance will be on your left.

Enter the park and turn left to get to the boat ramp.

Fees apply at this ramp and vary on weekdays, weekends or holidays.

This park has a very nice one-lane, paved ramp. Restrooms are available along with a picnic area and lots of paved parking.

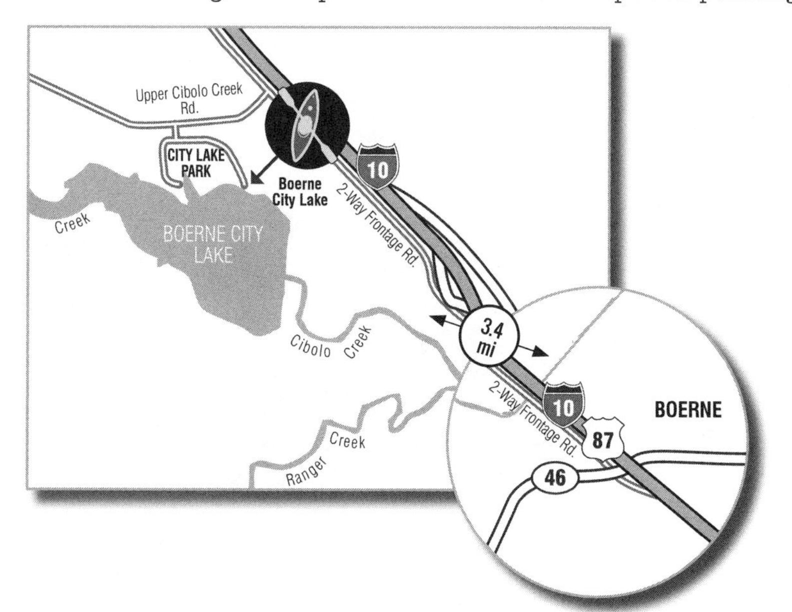

Coleto Creek

N 28 43.201, W 97 10.437 Elevation: 76 feet

From the intersection of U.S. Hwy 59 and U.S. Hwy 87 south of Victoria, Texas, continue south on 59, through the intersection of U.S. 59 with U.S. 77 and the intersection of U.S. 59/U.S. 77 and Bus. Hwy 59, a total of 16.5 miles to the park entrance. There are plenty of signs directing you here.

The park has a nice four-lane, boat ramp and plenty of bank space to launch from.

All the amenities are available here, restrooms, fishing pier, camping, playground and a spot for swimming.

This reservoir is a power plant cooling pond.

This is a fee-based park.

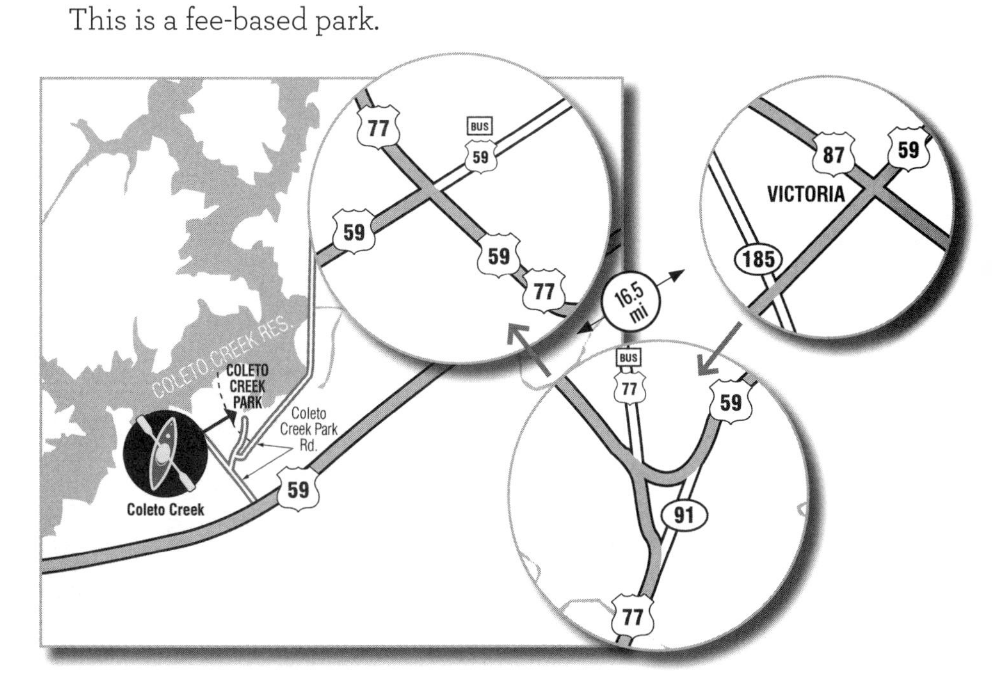